CONNECT MORE, LEAD MORE

Improve Your Connection Skills and
Become a Leader People Want to Follow

Bil Sadler

Contents

ACKNOWLEDGEMENTS

Writing a book is much harder than I ever thought! Although my name may be on the front cover, don't be fooled, I had lots of help.

First and foremost, I want to thank my wife, Heather. You listened to my ideas and ramblings and gave me your honest feedback. I know your feedback was honest because you didn't just agree with me—I really do appreciate that about you. Your never-ending, unconditional encouragement and support was the fire that kept me going. You rock!

To my three kids, Macy, Cole, and Layne Marie. You are truly a blessing in my life. And, your insights and humor provide me with great material!

To my dad, Gerald Sadler, who passed in 2014. It may not have seemed like it at the time, but I was listening. Thank you for sharing your wisdom with me.

To my mom, Joyce Sadler. Thank you for helping with the editing—I owe you! Also, thank you for all those little tent cards and notes you posted around the house when I was growing up. The quotes and Bible verses are still with me today.

To Kristy Thornton. Thank you for helping with the editing. I really appreciate you!

To my brother, Wes. I really appreciate your support, your wisdom, and your feedback. I bounce around a lot of ideas with you, and I know it can be overwhelming at times, but I can't imagine doing that with anyone else. By the way, you don't really owe me a nickel—I owe you much more.

And mostly, thank you God—it's not mine, it's yours.

INTRODUCTION

Honestly, leadership is kind of vague. So, what exactly is leadership? What makes someone a leader, or a good leader? How do you teach someone to be a leader?

For example, have you ever noticed someone who appeared to be a good leader? What did that person do to make you think he or she was a good leader? Was it just a feeling you had or was it something more specific? Was it because this person was in a leadership role? Did he or she present themselves well? Was it confidence, charisma, or character? Was he or she a good speaker or communicator?

Often, at least for me, it's difficult to put a finger on exactly what it is that makes a person a leader, much less, a good leader. But, when someone demonstrates leadership abilities, it's easy to recognize.

Why, then, is it difficult to quantify leadership into something specific? Most likely because leadership consists of soft skills. Whereas, hard skills such as accounting, payroll, nursing, web design, welding, painting, mechanics, cosmetology, construction, engineering, and even selling, can be readily learned, observed, and measured. Yet, with leadership how do you measure soft skills such as listening, communicating, and visioning?

One way to quantifiably measure a leader is through performance results (such as sales, customer or employee satisfaction, and project completion). Albeit, performance results are an indirect result of one's leadership effectiveness, there is an observable, strong correlation between the two.

With performance being a commonly accepted (and expected) measurement, many people seek to improve their leadership skills. The reasonable assumption is that developing leadership abilities may increase the probability of personally succeeding in life and/or business. This connection between leadership abilities and the probability of success provides certain people the necessary motivation to pursue personal leadership development on their own.

Although the connection between leadership development and personal success may seem fairly obvious, what is often overlooked is a connection between developing leaders, at all levels, within an organization and the success of that organization. An organization may be a business, non-profit, church, school, team, or any other entity with a pursuit of growth.

Developing leaders within an organization does not mean that every person is going to be in charge. It may mean, however, that every person may have increased responsibility. This increased responsibility, throughout the organization, is the fuel that drives growth. Why? As leadership ability increases, each person, on average, willingly takes on more, cares more, and serves more.

Is leadership worth developing on a personal level? Most would say, yes. Is leadership worth developing throughout an organization, even though leadership skills are considered soft skills? Absolutely!

Why wait for leaders to rise up when leaders can be trained up? Why reserve leadership training only for management or executives? Leaders come in all shapes and sizes and can benefit all aspects of an organization. The good news is that leadership begins with a few simple skills that can be learned and practiced by anyone, regardless of position on an organization chart.

Fundamentally, leadership is about people. Leadership occurs when people connect. In other words, people want to follow a leader with whom they feel a connection. This is where *Connect More, Lead More* comes in.

Connect More, Lead More is not a research book; it's a *practical application* book. Decades of research on leadership has already been done and there are some really great leadership books out there. This book is about *how to become a better leader by improving your ability to connect with others, on a business and personal level.*

Just One Chapter a Day for 31 Days

Connect More, Lead More has 31 chapters—one for each day if you treat it like a daily reading. Is it possible to improve your leadership skills in just one month? Heck yeah! I'm not saying you'll become the person in charge of your organization by next month. And I'm definitely not saying you'll become rich, nor own your own business in 31 days. What I am saying is that if you desire to become a better leader at work and/or at home, then learning leadership skills can improve your probability of success.

Thank you in advance for reading my book, *Connect More, Lead More*; I really appreciate it. Your comments and questions are welcomed as I am always open to making things better. Feel free to email me at bil@bilsadler.com.

Go ahead, lead the way.

1

IS LEADERSHIP LEARNABLE?

Anyone can improve their leadership abilities. Yes, anyone! That includes you and me.

Isn't that encouraging?

The first question we must answer (to make this book worthwhile) is: Are you *born* with leadership abilities or do you *learn* leadership abilities?

Many people say, "Oh, he's a natural born leader," or, "She was born to be a leader." Both statements imply that one is naturally born with leadership abilities and that it is not learned.

Is there any truth to being a natural born leader? Perhaps some.

Let's start with the obvious. Each person is different. Each person is born with a different personality. Each person grows up in a different environment, even if in the same household (that's a whole different subject we'll leave to the psychologists). And each person is born with different physical and mental abilities.

Starting with physical abilities, there are some people who are better at certain sports than others. Someone who is tall may be better at basketball or volleyball, simply because they are tall. Other body types may allow someone to be better at football, baseball, or track. Some people are more physically coordinated than others. The point is that you are born with a certain amount of physical ability. The level of physical ability you were born with may give you an advantage in certain areas. But this advantage is simply a head start.

What about mental abilities? Yes, some people are better at math, some are better at writing, and some are better at art or music. Some people are more mentally coordinated than others, allowing them to grasp things better or faster. Again, just like physical abilities, you are born with a certain amount of mental ability. Just like physical ability, the level of mental ability you were born with may give you an advantage in certain areas. But this

1

advantage is simply a head start.

Your leadership ability is no different. Some people are better at leading than others. Some people are better at public speaking, some are better at listening, and some are better at organizing. Each person is born with a certain amount of leadership ability, some more than others. The level of leadership ability you were born with may give you an advantage in certain areas. But this advantage is simply a head start.

For now, would you agree that each person is born with something and that "something" is in different amounts or levels? Can we agree that a person may be born with some natural ability that could give him or her a head start in certain areas?

Let's go back to the above statement, "He or she is a natural born leader." So let's say this person is a she, and she is in their thirties. You happen to be observing her speak to a group of people, perhaps at work. You are seeing and hearing her today, as she is today. She appears confident. She also appears to be a good, or even a great, leader. Was she born a great leader or did she develop her leadership skills?

A lot can happen in thirty something years. Unless you know this person on a personal level, how could you possibly know what this person has experienced? How could you know what training this person has pursued? How could you know what level of abilities she was born with and what level she developed? How could you know the depth of her desire to become a better leader? You couldn't. When you see someone demonstrating high-level skills or performance, whether in leadership, academics, sports, acting, or music, you couldn't possibly know how much hard work was invested to get to that high-level. If you don't know how much training and preparation was endured, you might assume this person is just naturally good.

Because you see this hypothetical person acting like a leader, whether it was natural or hard work got her there, we can make the assumption that she made a *choice* to use and develop her leadership skills. It's a choice because she could have said "No" to taking on leadership responsibilities. She could have chosen a different path. But in this example, the choice was to use her leadership abilities, including those that were natural and those that were developed.

What you do with your natural abilities is up to you.

➤ Will you use your abilities as they are, without further development? (Similar to the tall person playing basketball, yet not formally practicing or developing the fundamental skills to play basketball.)

➤ Will you use your abilities only when you need them, without further development? (Similar to the person who is willing and confident to get up and speak in front of a group, yet has no training in how to deliver a speech.)

➢ Do you have the desire to develop your natural abilities further? (Not everyone does, and that's okay.)

➢ Or will you choose not to use your abilities at all? (Similar to the person who can sing, yet chooses not to.)

How you use your natural abilities is your choice; totally your choice. And whatever you decide to do with your abilities is okay. You may be built like a football running back, but what if you don't want to play football? It's okay. You may be built like a basketball center, forward, or guard, but what if you don't want to play basketball? It's okay. You may have a great mind for math, but what if you don't want to be on the math team or be an accountant or a NASA engineer? It's okay. What if you're musically inclined, but have no desire to play an instrument? That's okay too. It's your choice.

Ultimately, there is a powerful force that will determine which path you take—and that force is your internal desire. You will pursue that which you desire. The first question is, "What do you desire most?" The second question is, "How bad do you want it?" If you know what you want and you want it bad enough, it doesn't matter if you were born with certain abilities or not, you will do what it takes to develop the necessary skills. Another person may have more natural ability than you, therefore this person has a head start. But if that person doesn't further develop their natural abilities, for whatever reason, then you could easily surpass them by developing yours. Do you have the desire? Do you want it bad enough?

Did you know that Michael Jordan, one of basketball's all-time greats, didn't make the high school basketball team during his sophomore tryout? He was 15 years old, only 5'10", and couldn't yet dunk a basketball. He could've given up, but he didn't—he chose to develop his skills. Jordan spent his tenth grade year working out, and growing. According to a *Newsweek Special Edition* (October 17, 2015) article, Michael Jordan not only made the high school team in his junior year, but he became the team's best player and was named McDonald's All-American. If you're familiar with Michael Jordan, then you know the rest of the story.

What about great musicians? Do great musicians come out of the womb knowing how to play a guitar, piano, or any other instrument? No, no, no. Their natural abilities may have given them a head start, but it takes at least some level of instruction and a deep desire to become truly great at anything.

What about leadership? You don't have to become a great leader or even *the* leader. Some people simply don't want anything to do with being a leader, much less *the* leader. However, as you'll soon learn, leadership skills can help you at work in your present position; at home in your present relationships; and in pursuing whatever it is that you desire.

So, can you learn leadership? Here's research that proves you can.

In the book *Learning Leadership*, James M. Kouzes and Barry Z. Posner provide research supporting that leadership is learnable. A Florida State University professor, K. Anders Ericsson, found, over 30 years of research, that it takes more than raw talent to become a top performer. Regardless of the field, including leadership, it is not talent that is the key to excellence, but a set of learnable skills. Further, what separates expert performers from good performers is being committed to daily improvement. Becoming the best takes hard work and practice.

This is great news! How can anyone argue with over 30 years of research? Becoming a leader is a methodical process that you can work on daily. It won't happen overnight, but you will be surprised how quickly it can happen.

The truth is, however, that most people aren't willing to do the hard work necessary to improve at anything, even if they have some natural abilities to give them a head start. This is also good news for you. Why? Because, if you are willing to do the hard work, this leaves more room for you and others who will do what it takes to rise to the top.

It begins with desire. If you have the desire to improve your leadership skills and abilities, then you can, if you will.

If, indeed, leadership is a learnable set of skills and abilities, and you have the desire, then follow these three steps:

1. The first step is to learn what those skills and abilities are—through *reading*.
2. The second step is to develop your leadership skills and abilities— through *training*.
3. And the third step is applying and practicing your skills and abilities in real life—*at work, at home, and in public*.

Can we agree that developing your leadership skills is a choice, your choice? Can we also agree that using your leadership skills is your choice?

If you so choose—leadership is learnable.

Questions for Growth

1. Do you have a desire to improve your leadership abilities?
2. What leadership abilities do you feel you were born with, whether refined or not?
3. What leadership skills would you like to develop?
4. What books have you read to help understand and develop your leadership skills?
5. What seminars or training have you taken to develop your leadership skills?
6. Do you desire to be a leader? If so, describe your leadership aspirations.

References and Sources:

o   Kouzes, James M. And Posner, Barry Z., *Learning Leadership: The Five Fundamentals of Becoming an Exemplary Leader* (Wiley 2016), 5, 10. Kouzes and Posner reference the following: Geoff Colvin, *Talent Is Overrated: What Really Separates World-Class Performers from Everybody Else* (New York: Penguin Group, 2010); Daniel Coyle, *The Talent Code: Greatness Isn't Born. It's Grown. Here's How* (New York: Bantam Dell, 2009). Also, K. Anders Ericsson, ed., *The Road to Excellence: The Acquisition of Expert Performance in the Arts and Sciences, Sports, and Games* (Mahwah, NJ: Lawrence Erlbaum Associates, 1996); K. Anders Ericsson, ed., *Development of Expert Performance and Design of Optimal Learning* (New York: Cambridge University Press, 2009).

o   *Newsweek Special Edition*, (October 17, 2015) Article: *Michael Jordan Didn't Make Varsity-At First.*

2
WHAT IS LEADERSHIP?

Leadership is often associated with a position of leadership, such as a manager, owner, CEO, COO, CFO, team (department, division, or group) leader, director, pastor, teacher, coach, or parent. All of these examples are *positions* of leadership, but do not actually define leadership.

Leadership does not come from your position; leadership comes from within you. For example, any player on a football team can be put in the game to play the position of quarterback. Does that make him a quarterback? Of course not. He may have the title because of the position, but he must possess the mindset, ability, and skill to actually be a quarterback.

Similarly, the position (within a business or organization context) does not make a person a leader. The position may give you the title, but it does not make you a leader, particularly a good leader. The person makes the leader. *You* make the leader.

If leadership is not a position, then what is it?

Let's look at some definitions.

According to Dictionary.com, *leadership* (noun) is:
1) the position or function of a leader, a person who guides or directs a group;
2) ability to lead;
3) an act or instance of leading; guidance; direction;
4) the leaders of a group.

From this definition it's easy to see why leadership is often associated with a *position* of leadership. Note that leadership is a noun which is a person, place, or thing. Therefore, leadership as a noun must be a person or a position. So let's look at the word *lead* from which leadership is derived. *Lead* is a verb. A verb expresses an action typically performed by the noun: *The leader (noun) leads (action) the group.*

Again from Dictionary.com, *lead* (verb) is:
1) to go before or with, to show the way;
2) to conduct by holding and guiding;
3) to influence or induce;
4) to guide in direction, course, action, opinion.

The various definitions of *lead* are actually much longer, but with similar descriptions, so we'll stop here. The point is that the *action* of a leader is *what* a leader does. And it is this action that actually makes a leader, not the position.

For comparison, in football you can have good quarterbacks, great quarterbacks, and not-so-great quarterbacks. The actions of a quarterback are what set them apart from one another. Similarly, you can have good leaders, great leaders, and not-so-great leaders. The actions of a leader are what set them apart from one another as well.

The actions of a leader will be our focus in this book. Specifically, your actions reflect how you affect others. And *how* you affect others is your ability to influence others. Consider the following.

➢ In 1936 Dale Carnegie published *How to Win Friends and Influence People.* Carnegie uses the word *influence* to describe leadership.

➢ John Maxwell also describes leadership as *influence* in his book *Leadership 101.*

The definition (Dictionary.com) of *influence* (verb) is:
1) to exercise influence on (to be a compelling force on the actions, behavior, opinions, etc., of others);
2) to move or impel (a person) to some action.

In addition, here are some synonyms for influence: *alter, authority, control, direction, effect, guide, impact, inspire, model, power, shape, sway, transform.*

Based on everything that I've studied so far, I believe the best way to describe leadership is, indeed, *influence.*

Please note, influence can be positive or negative. Without belaboring the point, I hope it's clear that I am influencing you in a *positive* direction when it comes to becoming a better leader. (Just making sure we're on the same page.)

Leadership involves three main areas of development:
➢ **Mindset** - The attitude, intention, or inclination for leading.
➢ **Ability** - The capacity, competence, or aptitude for leading.
➢ **Skill** - How well you perform certain actions for leading.

Ideally you want to develop all three areas. The better your mindset, ability, and skill, the better leader you can become. Think of improving each of these areas as exercising. The more you exercise, the stronger or healthier you become.

For example, for many years I worked behind a desk in an office environment. By all measures I lived a sedentary lifestyle. I'd go to work and go home, with little or no exercise. In my 40s my biometric numbers began to show higher cholesterol and blood pressure. Besides that, my body weight was creeping up. All those years I knew that exercise was important, I just didn't consider it to be urgent. When my numbers began to creep up I began to see the urgency.

At age 49 I decided to start jogging. I decided on jogging because of something I learned in my teens from one of my lawn mowing customers, Mr. Rogers. It seemed like Mr. Rogers was going for a run every time I mowed his lawn. One day I asked if he ran marathons. He said, "No, I run just one mile every day, weather permitting."

This was not the answer I expected. "Why just one mile?" I asked.

He said, "Because it keeps me healthy." His answer stayed with me and at age 49 I decided to take up jogging.

What does this have to do with becoming a better leader?

I was influenced by Mr. Rogers. His positive actions and words had an impact on me that I remembered almost 35 years later. He was being a leader to me and probably didn't even realize it. Of course, I didn't realize the value at the time either.

Make no mistake about it, you are an influence to someone. Therefore, you are leading, perhaps unintentionally. But, no matter how impossible it may seem, you can become a better leader, intentionally. The more you do the actions that leaders do, the better you will become. Don't worry about how small the actions are, just do them.

If you are already a good leader, you can become an even better leader. If you're a great leader, well maybe it's time to expand your leadership into helping others become better leaders.

What's the takeaway?

Leadership is your positive influence on others. And no matter where you are right now, you can become a better leader by regularly doing the things that leaders do.

And that is the subject of the next section—doing the things that leaders do.

Questions for Growth

1. Name one person who has influenced you.
2. How did this person influence you?
3. Are there others?
4. Who are some of the people around you at home, work, or other?
5. How would you describe your influence on others?
6. Do you consider yourself a leader? Why or why not?
7. Are you open to improving as a leader?

BIL SADLER

References and Sources:

o   Dictionary.com
o   Carnegie, Dale, *How to Win Friends and Influence People* (Pocket Books, a division of Simon and Schuster, Inc., 1982).
o   Maxwell, John, *Leadership 101* (Thomas Nelson, Inc., 2002), page ix.

3

SMALL STEPS

Nothing is particularly hard if you divide it into small jobs. Henry Ford

When I was a teenager my mom used to place quotes on little tent cards around the house—particularly on the bathroom vanity where I'd have to see it several times a day. One quote that sort of sounded like a riddle still sticks with me to this day:

Little and often make a lot.

Honestly, I didn't think much about it at first. But one day while doing my homework, something clicked. Rather than waiting until the day before an assignment was due, I'd do a little studying each day. I found that doing a little every day was much easier than doing a lot at one time. This also made it easier to study for a test and to prepare note cards, if necessary.

Another application of this quote is reading. I don't have time to read a 200 to 300 page book. At times I've been overwhelmed by the thought of reading a lengthy book—to the point of not reading it at all. However, I *can* read five to ten pages per day. In a month, that's 150 to 300 pages. That would be twelve books per year; not too bad for someone who doesn't have time to read.

While walking for miles and miles behind a lawn mower as a teenager, I had plenty of thinking time. The more I thought about *little and often make a lot*, the more I saw how it applied to almost everything. Other than reading a book, here are a few more examples:

➢ Exercising
➢ Saving for retirement
➢ Reading the Bible (Reading just one chapter a day, it took me three and half years, but I actually read the whole Bible!)
➢ Changing eating habits

> ➢ Learning a new skill, hobby, or a musical instrument
> ➢ Improving communication in a relationship

Besides these personal areas, *little and often make a lot* can also be applied to leadership development. Becoming a leader doesn't happen overnight. In fact, becoming a great leader can take years, even decades. However, becoming a better leader can start today.

To see how this works, let's dissect this quote, *little / and often / make a lot.*

Little—Whatever the task, it doesn't have to be huge. In fact, the bigger the task, the less likely I would actually do it. For example, I tried reading the Bible through in a year, but that required reading three or four chapters a day—too big of a task for me. Smaller tasks, however, are easier to perform. Continuing the Bible example, I could read one chapter a day with no problem—it usually only took ten minutes.

Why does this work? Small tasks require very little thinking, decision making, or completion time—they're so small, you just do it. Typically, we tend to challenge ourselves by increasing the things we do, like exercising— if we did 10 push-ups yesterday, then we increase the goal to do more the next day. After a while of increasing, many tasks become drudgery. If you find this happening with any of your routines, back it down to a ridiculously small goal that requires very little effort. If you do more than your small goal, that's fine, but keep your minimum requirement low. You're more likely to do a small task than a large one.

Often—As I brainstormed the word *often*, two words kept coming to mind—consistent and persistent. According to Dictionary.com, *consistent* means "adhering to the same principles, course, form, etc." And *persistent* means "to continue steadfastly or firmly in some state, purpose, course of action, especially in spite of opposition, obstacles, discouragement; lasting or enduring tenaciously." In other words, being consistent and persistent means performing the same task, activity, or habit on a regular basis in spite of obstacles. However, what I found to be true for me, the smaller the task, the smaller the obstacles.

Make a lot—By performing a small task often, something amazing begins to happen over time. You may not notice much at first, but over time results begin to show. The more time that passes, the greater the results. Picture someone taking guitar lessons for the first time—awkward. If the student practices just 15 minutes a day, small improvements would accumulate, although unnoticeable on a daily basis. If you were to take a short video of the guitar student playing the same song every day for 30 days, then watch these videos back to back, surely you would see noticeable improvement from beginning to end.

One day it all kind of came together for me when I realized why I, and many others, aren't as consistent and persistent as we could be. I believe it's because we're focusing on big, rather than small tasks. For example, we make our goals and resolutions too big to be realistic. A New Year's resolution of working out two hours a day, when you haven't been working out at all, just isn't realistic. A goal of eating only vegan foods, when you've been eating a typical American diet, just isn't realistic. We naturally have a tendency to bite off more than we can chew—we want the big payoff now, not later.

Self-discipline seems to be difficult for many people, including myself. Naturally, self-discipline can become even more difficult when the repetitive task is too big or takes too much time. However, you can improve your self-discipline by making your daily activities smaller, much smaller. If it's exercising, rather than two hours per day, try 15 minutes a day. If every day is too much, try three days per week.[1] If it's eating healthier, try one healthy meal per day.[1] The point is, you don't have to do big things to be a self-disciplined person. You can be self-disciplined by doing small things, consistently. Doing such small things may feel like cheating, but who cares! You're more likely to do smaller things than bigger things. In other words, it's better to do smaller things frequently than to do bigger things infrequently or to quit. So what? Well, if you'll do the smaller things on a daily basis, you'll find yourself becoming more self-disciplined, even if you don't consider yourself a disciplined person.

I was always taught that my goals had to be big; I needed to think big, and dream big. While that sounds good, it doesn't always stick—it's not usually sustainable. Rather, I found that writing down these big goals and dreams helps to establish a target. But to get there, I needed to focus on the activities or steps that would take me in the direction of my target. These activities and steps are the *habits* required to get you where you want to go. And the cool thing is, they don't have to be all that big—they can be small habits, in fact, very small habits. The important thing is to actually do the activities and steps. If your activities and steps are small enough, you're more likely to do them every day, without fail and without much thinking. If you're having difficulties making it happen, then make your steps smaller—ridiculously small if necessary.

The bottom line—the more you do something, even if it's ridiculously small, the more comfortable you'll become; and you're more likely to stick to it and accomplish more in the long-run. Here's an example my dad taught me.

When I was a teenager I would spend money as fast as it came to me. My dad challenged me to save just one dollar for every lawn I mowed (back then I made about $10 per lawn). I said, "Dad, that's ridiculous, what good is that gonna do?"

He said, "Each week I want you to go to the bank and make a deposit, no matter how small, into your savings account. Will you promise me you'll do that?"

I agreed.

When I got out of school and started working full-time, I finally realized what happened. Dad taught me to form the habit of saving money, one ridiculously small deposit at a time.

Little and often make a lot.

Often we're told to jump right in and face our fears. In certain situations, facing your fears by jumping in can and will work. If jumping in works for you, and that's what you feel most comfortable with, then go ahead and jump in.

However, if jumping in doesn't work or hasn't worked for you, perhaps a different approach might be better. Take a slower approach, with itty-bitty, teeny-weeny, baby steps. Here's how it works.

What does your brain do when faced with a fear? My brain tells me to run for my life! It's the fight or flight instinct.

But what if you bypassed your brain's fear altogether? You can. Simply make the steps toward your goal extremely small. It's like gradually stepping in the cold swimming pool one inch per step. It may take an hour to actually get in the pool, but you avoid the shock and fear of jumping in the cold water. Once you're totally in the swimming pool, you're acclimated to the cold water and you avoided the shock. It's not a matter of which method is faster or better, *it's a matter of which one you will actually do.* If the fear of jumping in the pool will prevent you from getting in the pool, then gradually step in—don't avoid the pool altogether.[2]

Not only will *little and often make a lot* help in your work life, it can also help in your personal life—exercising, eating, saving, retirement, debt reduction, relationships, etc.

The reason *little and often make a lot* works is because the steps you take each day are so small, you barely have to think about doing it; you just do it. Each day you become more accustomed to performing the step, and as a result you become desensitized to any fears or overwhelm. On some days you may feel like doing more than your minimum step. Great! Take advantage of your energy and do more. However, don't change your minimum small step for the next day. Keep it low. If you can do more, fine. If not, just do the minimum.

The idea is to form a lasting habit that will move you toward your goal. Habits are formed through repetition—repeating the same thing, at the same time, using the same method. Make your small steps part of your daily routine.

As you go through this book, look for the small activities you can start practicing now. Don't worry about how well you can perform a task, just practice and you will improve.

Remember, becoming a better leader doesn't happen overnight; it's a process. And becoming a better leader is not a destination; it's a journey. Great leaders continue the process and enjoy the journey.

All leaders, great and small, had a beginning. Becoming a better leader has to begin somewhere and at some time. I'm not sure where I heard this quote, seems like Warren Buffett said something similar, or it may be a Chinese Proverb:

The best time to plant a beautiful oak tree is 50 years ago.
The next best time is today.

[1.] Exercising just 15 minutes per day for three days a week, or eating just one healthy meal per day, may not seem like much, but look around, who's doing even that? If you did this minimum amount for just one year, heck, even one quarter, you'll make significant improvements. I know it doesn't seem like much, or maybe it doesn't seem like you're punishing yourself enough to actually work, but it does. I dare you to try it.

[2.] If your goal is to skydive, for whatever reason, you can't tip-toe out of the plane; I'm sorry, but you just have to jump.

Questions for Growth

1. How do you feel about doing small tasks or habits, such as exercising just 15 minutes per day for three days per week, or eating just one healthy meal per day?
2. What is one thing you would like to accomplish, and maybe you've tried, but have been unsuccessful at achieving?
3. How could you use *little and often make a lot* to help with your pursuit?
4. Do you believe it works?
5. Do you believe it will work for you?
6. Using this small step principle, what is one thing you'd be willing to try?
7. How could you use this principle to improve your leadership skills?
8. Would you consider reading one of the books listed below in the References and Sources to get a better understanding of how this principle works?

References and Sources:
o   Dictionary.com
o   Guise, Stephen, *Mini Habits: Smaller Habits, Bigger Results (Volume 1),* (CreateSpace

Independent Publishing Platform, 2013)

o   Hardy, Daren, *The Compound Effect: Jumpstart Your Income, Your Life, Your Success,* (Vanguard Press, 2012)
o   Maurer Ph.D, Robert, *One Small Step Can Change Your Life: The Kaizen Way,* (Workman Publishing Company, Inc., 2004)
o   Maurer Ph.D, Robert, *The Spirit of Kaizen: Creating Lasting Excellence One Small Step at a Time,* (McGraw-Hill Education, 2012)

4

THE TWO YOU'S

People are where they are because that is exactly where they really want to be—whether they will admit that or not. Earl Nightingale

Did you know there are two versions of yourself?

First, there is your current self. Your current self is who you are right now. It's how you currently think; it's how you currently do things; it's the decisions you currently make and the way you go about making decisions. It's how you eat, how you exercise, how you speak—it's every habit you have whether good or bad. Your current self is also your physical appearance, including the clothes you wear and the way you do your hair. It's you—it's everything about you just as you are at this very moment.

The other you is your desired self. This is how you would like to be, look, and act.

What does your desired self look like? Following are self-assessment questions to get you started.

- ➢ How well does your desired self listen?
- ➢ How well does your desired self communicate?
- ➢ How well does your desired self respond/react?
- ➢ How patient is your desired self?
- ➢ Is your desired self concerned about others?
- ➢ How well does your desired self help others?
- ➢ How well does your desired self think before speaking?
- ➢ How well does your desired self take criticism?
- ➢ How does your desired self dress?
- ➢ How does your desired self look physically?
- ➢ How does your desired self exercise?

➤ How healthy is your desired self?
➤ What does your desired self need to learn?
➤ What position does your desired self hold?
➤ Is your desired self comfortable with public speaking?
➤ How disciplined is your desired self?
➤ What positive habits does your desired self possess?
➤ What negative habits does your desired self need to eliminate?
➤ Where does your desired self live?
➤ Describe the financial situation of your desired self.
➤ What are the financial habits of your desired self?
➤ How well does your desired self get along with others?
➤ How well does your desired self encourage others?
➤ How trustworthy is your desired self?

Okay, these are just a handful of questions to get you thinking about your desired self. Now, I'd like to share a personal example of physical appearance and health to illustrate this concept of current self and desired self.

My current self weighed 216 pounds and my blood pressure and cholesterol numbers were borderline high. Although I'm tall and people say I can "carry my weight well," I wasn't happy with the inner tube around my waist. I didn't feel healthy. I ate pretty much whatever I wanted and I didn't exercise at all. Two things got my attention. First, my doctor wanted me to start taking a small dose of cholesterol medication. He said this was "normal" as someone ages and puts on weight. Second, I saw a picture of myself sitting in a beach chair on a family vacation. Oh man! Did I really look like that? I vowed to never take my shirt off again at the beach.

Something had to change. Like most of my planning, I used reverse-engineering. I wrote a description of what I wanted to look like—this was my desired self. My desired self weighed in the 190's with a normal blood pressure and cholesterol. My desired self felt healthy.

Then, I came up with the steps it would take to get from my current self, weighing 216 pounds, to my desired self, weighing 195 pounds. These steps became the habits of my desired self.

What were the habits of my desired self?
1. Eat smaller portions
2. Eat more vegetables
3. Eat more fruits
4. Eat less processed foods
5. Eat less meat
6. Eat less sugar
7. Eat less bread
8. Drink more water
9. Avoid soft drinks

10. Exercise regularly

Okay, this is not a recommendation of an ideal diet, this is what I came up with for me. The point is that my desired self had certain habits that made the desired self into the healthy person, happy person I desired. If I wanted to transform from my current self into my desired self, then I had to actually do the things my desired self would do.

As I got into action, I found that the above list was kind of vague, so I had to get more specific about the habits of my desired self. Here are a few examples:

1. For breakfast my desired self drinks smoothies or eats old fashioned rolled oats with sunflower seeds, raisins, and fruit.
2. For lunch my desired self eats a salad. This kept me from feeling sluggish in the afternoon.
3. For supper my desired self eats a salad and perhaps a small portion of lean meat such as salmon or grilled chicken.
4. Keep a glass of water at my desk so I could sip on it throughout the day.
5. My desired self jogs for 15 minutes per day for three to five days per week.
6. My desired self does three sets of ten push-ups for three days per week.

Notice how these habits are much more specific. I knew exactly what I needed to do and what groceries I needed to have on hand. Am I always perfect? Of course not.

This concept can be applied to just about any area of your life—work, career, where you live, financial situation, attitude, health, relationships, and, of course, leadership.

Many leaders are good communicators, particularly when it comes to public speaking. Yet, many people have a fear of public speaking. If this applies you, why not include public speaking in the description of your desired self? Imagine your desired self speaking in front of a group of people. Imagine your confidence and competence. Imagine how well you've prepared and rehearsed. Imagine that you sincerely want to help your audience. Imagine that your focus is on your audience and not on yourself. Imagine yourself carrying on a conversation with your audience. Imagine your audience laughing and enjoying your entertainment. If there is one skill that can move you further than just about any other, it is definitely public speaking.

Once you come up with a picture of your desired self, make a list of specific habits that your desired self would do in order to be the person you desire to be. If it helps, write these habits on an index card and carry it with you as a constant reminder.

As you go through your day think about the things you do and ask,

"What would my desired self do in this situation?" Do your best to do *more* of the things that your desired self would do, and *less* of the things your current self would do. (It's not about being perfect, it's about making progress.) Soon you'll find that you are becoming more like your desired self. The more you do what your desired self would do, the more you'll actually become your desired self.

Exercise - Divide a sheet of paper into three equal vertical columns. Label the first column "Current Self." Label the third column "Desired Self." Label the middle column "Steps to get there."

1. In the "Current Self" column, write down everything you can think of about how you currently are.
2. In the "Desired Self" column, write down everything you can think of about how you'd like to be.
3. In the "Steps to get there" column, write down the specific habits that your desired self would do.
4. Reduce the "Steps to get there" to an index card and carry it around with you as a reminder to develop the habits to become your desired self.

One of my examples was the desire to be an author. One of the steps to get there was to write for 15 to 30 minutes per day. I kept asking myself what would an author do? The answer was always, "Write."

Questions for Growth

1. Using what you wrote in the above exercise, how would you describe your current self?
2. How would you describe your desired self?
3. How would your desired self act differently?
4. Is there an area in your life (such as work, career, where you live, financial situation, attitude, health, relationships, leadership) in which you are dissatisfied and you desire to change?
5. What are you willing to do?

5

IT'S ALL ABOUT RELATIONSHIPS

There is no leadership without people. To be a leader there must be at least one other person with whom you share your influence.

I've heard people say, "I'll be glad to help any way I can, but I'm just not a leader."

While they may think this is true, in reality, what they really mean is that they don't *want* to be the person in charge (or take responsibility). However, everyone is a leader to some degree. Are you in a committed relationship? Are you a parent? Do you have siblings? Do you have friends? Do you work around others? Do you have customers or clients? If you answered "yes" to any of these questions, then you are a leader. You may not think of yourself as a leader if you're relating leadership to being the person in charge. And, there may very well be another person who is the dominate person in your relationships, but leadership is not just a position— leadership is influence and it goes in both directions.

You do not have to be the person in charge to be a leader. For example, in football the head coach is in charge. However, there is usually a player who consistently shares enthusiasm and encourages his teammates. Even though this player is not in charge, he is influencing the other players.

Let's say you're on a team at work and there is a team leader who is in charge. This team leader provides guidance for a particular project. Even if you're not the team leader, you can be a leader for others on the team in many ways:

- ➤ Encourage others
- ➤ Train others
- ➤ Set an example
- ➤ Be flexible
- ➤ Facilitate the process
- ➤ Be available for assistance

> ➢ Share a positive attitude
> ➢ Be optimistic
> ➢ Show support

If you share your influence with others, then you are a leader. Therefore, anyone who has relationships is a leader because you can't be in a relationship without influencing the other person(s) in the relationship.

Leadership fosters healthy relationships, both business and personal. Leadership helps relationships develop, improve, grow, and branch. In fact, it's all about relationships. Leadership *is* the influence of others.

So when we talk about leadership in this book, we're talking about improving your ability to influence others in a positive direction. And as you grow in your ability to influence, your relationships will grow. Not only can you improve your existing relationships, but you can develop new relationships as well.

Leadership—it's all about relationships!

Relationships are important to a leader. It's very difficult for a leader to go to work in a bubble without interacting with anyone. How can a leader influence someone without interaction? That would be difficult, if not impossible. Perhaps you've heard someone say, "I wish they'd just leave me alone and let me do my job." Maybe the person said this because they really are extremely busy. But in many cases, it's not because they're busy, it's because they don't want to interact with others. Can the person who wants to be left alone be a leader? It's possible, but not likely. Something needs to change to be a leader and it's primarily your interaction with others.

In general, interaction with others has three different levels.

1. On the surface—Information exchange
2. Below surface—Discussion of thoughts
3. Deep—Exploration of emotions

As you interact with others, think about the level of your interaction. This doesn't mean you should have, or even strive, for a deep interaction with everyone you come in contact with. At this point it's simply a matter of awareness. Some relationships will never get below the surface. However, other relationships may be operating on the surface, but require deeper exploration.

Moving a relationship from one level to another is a gradual process. Take dating for example. You get to know someone on the surface first. Gradually, you become more comfortable with one another and the relationship moves below the surface.[1] For the dating relationship to grow and last, there needs to be a deeper emotional connection. Don't rush the process, let it grow by peeling the onion one layer at a time.

Improving your ability to interact with others depends on your ability to *connect* with others. What does it mean to connect? The definition of *connect* (Dictionary.com) is "to establish communication between; to cause to be associated as in a business or personal relationship; to associate mentally or emotionally."

So, how well do you connect with others?

The premise of this book is about your ability to connect—the better you can connect, the better you can lead. And that's what helped determine the book's name—*Connect More, Lead More*.

Although "Leadership" involves many competencies, I believe your ability to connect is the fundamental component to your growth as a leader. The better you can connect with others, the better opportunity you'll have to learn and grow as a leader. People like to follow someone they can relate to or connect with.

If you've ever played sports, you know there are certain fundamentals that you practice over and over. These fundamentals are the most basic skills needed to play the game. For example, in basketball there are dribbling, passing, and shooting skills. There are fundamental skills in football, soccer, baseball, volleyball, swimming, track, and every other sport. Learning the fundamentals is required to play the game. The better you are at the fundamentals, the better you can play the game.

Interestingly, you can become good at the fundamentals in sports, yet not be very good at connecting with your teammates. The same applies to your work—you can be technically proficient at your work, yet not be very good at connecting with your co-workers. Developing as a leader, if that's what you want, requires more than being good at your job. You may possess and excel at all the technical skills required for your job, but to grow as a leader you must improve your ability to connect with others.

Have you ever seen the movie *Jerry Maguire* with Tom Cruise, Renee Zellweger, and Cuba Gooding, Jr.? Tom Cruise played Jerry Maguire, a sports agent. Maguire's only client was Rod Tidwell (Cuba Gooding, Jr.), a wide receiver for the Arizona Cardinals. Tidwell was a talented wide receiver and wanted more money. He kept telling Jerry to "Show me the money!" Paraphrasing, Jerry's response was that Tidwell was not worthy of more money—he was only focused on the money and himself. In essence, Tidwell didn't play well with others, including the fans, players, and coaches. Near the end of the movie Tidwell got hurt and passed out, during which he had a revelation. As he regained consciousness, he got up, danced around on the field, and showed love to the fans. This was Tidwell's turning point where he connected with others.

You can have all the skills and all the smarts in the world, but it takes more than that to become a good leader—you must be able to connect with others.

In the following chapters you'll learn various relationship skills to improve your ability to connect with others. And it all starts with you.

[1.] By the way, we're talking about communication here, not something physical.

Questions for Growth

1. Are you in a leadership position in your work, specifically leading others?
2. Are you good at what you do, technically speaking?
3. How well do you connect with others?
4. Whether you connect well with others or not, what makes this so?
5. Are you willing to improve your ability to connect?
6. What can you do to improve?

6
IT ALL STARTS WITH YOU

When we think of leadership we generally think about leading others. But, before you can lead others, you must be able to lead yourself—it all starts with you.

How do you lead yourself?

The first step in leading yourself is self-awareness. This is not easy. It's much easier to look at and critique others than it is to look inward and critique yourself. However, to grow as a leader and a person, becoming self-aware is not optional.

Self-awareness can start with a general assessment of yourself. Draw a line down the middle of a single sheet of paper. Write "Strengths" on the left and "Weaknesses" on the right. Ideally, get in a quiet place so you can think without interruption. At first, just list the things you consider to be your strengths and weaknesses. What are you good at and what do you need to work on?

To dig a little deeper, reflect on your past experiences. In particular, think about the people in your life. What experiences can you recall? What happened? What did the other person do? What did you do? As you think about your experiences, don't focus as much on what others did or didn't do, focus on you and how you responded. How did you react? How did you help? How did you hurt? Look for your strengths and weaknesses and continue to write them on your list.

Going even deeper with this exercise, what would others say are your strengths and weaknesses? Would they say you're a good listener? Would they say you speak before you think? Would they say you talk about yourself too much? Would they say you don't seem to be concerned with others? Perhaps you don't have to guess because people have actually told you how you are. Has anyone ever called you a jerk? Has more than one person called you a jerk? Could there be some truth in your actually being a

25

jerk? Maybe just a little? Looking at yourself from the perspective of what others would say, continue to write down your strengths and weaknesses.

If you really want some feedback, consider asking a few people for their opinion/critique of you. Ask for good points and bad points. Don't just pop in and ask them to spout off a critique of you on the spot. Let them know you'd like their honest opinion, then give them a few days to think about it. Their response could be done verbally or written, depending on how comfortable the other person feels. It's ultra-important for you to make it safe for them to respond honestly. Tell them you're looking for honest feedback and that you won't react or respond except to clarify. Now, whatever you do, don't get defensive and don't react. Simply thank them for being honest and let them know you are trying to grow.

What do you think so far? Are you satisfied with your strengths? Are there areas you could improve?

The second step is to do a more formal assessment of your personality and behavior. Two popular assessments are Myers-Briggs Type Indicator® and DISC® Profile. Another assessment not quite as formal is the shape personality test. These assessments are not tests, they just tell you about yourself. There are no right or wrong answers; they're your answers.

The third step is to create a personal development plan to build on your strengths. For example, continuing the football analogy, if you're a good quarterback, then work on your quarterback skills. There's no need to practice kicking, punting, or snapping. Focus on your strengths and do them well.

Generally, you'll have two types of weaknesses. One type of weakness is simply something that you're not that good at, like organizing, for example. Although it would be good to improve your ability to organize, this type of weakness won't necessarily hold you back. In the football example, even though the quarterback is not good at kicking, punting, or snapping, these weaknesses will not hold him back from being an excellent quarterback.

The other type of weakness is an obstacle that must be overcome or else the weakness will hold you back. A good example is poor listening skills. A leader needs to possess good listening skills just as a quarterback needs to possess good passing skills.

Examine your weaknesses and determine which you need to improve to become a better leader.

Your ability to self-assess is critical for your growth. Awareness, as we've discussed thus far, is only the first step, but it's an important step. Just being aware of, or educated about, something can lead to positive improvement. The increased awareness/knowledge influences your behavior ever so slightly. However, once you're aware of an area that needs improvement, it's time to do something about it. In the following chapters we'll look at various personal development areas that are important to leadership. Not only will we look at them, but you'll learn practical ideas on how to improve.

At this point, begin critiquing yourself on how you handle day-to-day situations. How do you respond to those around you? How do you respond under stress? How do you respond when someone asks you for help? After each interaction take a moment to debrief yourself. What just happened and how did you respond?

From a 30,000 foot view, the main thing you're striving for is *self-control*--physically and emotionally.

Questions for Growth

1. Based on your self-assessment, how would you describe yourself?
2. What are your strengths?
3. What are your weaknesses?
4. Has anyone ever told you how you are, or aren't? (Jerk, poor listener, talk too much, etc.)
5. Have you asked for feedback from someone who knows you? If not, are you willing to ask?
6. Have you ever taken a personality test? If so, describe your results. Did you agree with your assessment?
7. What is a weakness of yours that won't necessarily hold you back?
8. What is a weakness of yours that, if not improved, will hold you back?
9. What is a strength of yours that you need to improve further?
10. How would you describe your self-control?

7

THE RELATIONSHIP GLUE

In the past couple of chapters we've talked about leadership from a people perspective—leadership is your ability to influence others, as well as yourself. Your ability to influence others will be based on your ability to connect with others, in other words, *Connect More, Lead More.*

To connect with others there is one thing that must be in place—it's the glue that holds relationships together. What is this relationship glue?

TRUST

Trust comes before people skills. Without trust, no one will voluntarily follow your leadership.

What is trust?

Here are some words often used to describe *trust:*

- ➢ Ability
- ➢ Assurance
- ➢ Character
- ➢ Commitment
- ➢ Confidence
- ➢ Consistency
- ➢ Faith
- ➢ Hope
- ➢ Integrity
- ➢ Reliance
- ➢ Respect
- ➢ Responsibility
- ➢ Safety
- ➢ Steadfastness
- ➢ Strength
- ➢ Surety

Although these words describe trust, it's kind of difficult to say exactly what it is or what you can do to build trust. If I had to boil it down to a definition that I could share with my kids I'd say that *trust is the confidence that others have in you to do the right thing.*

Trust is something you earn. Some people may give you their trust at first, and others won't trust you until you're proven trustworthy. Either way, you must work to earn, prove, and maintain trust.

Trust is fragile. It takes time to develop trust, yet it can be broken in an instant. Once trust is broken it is difficult, if not impossible, to rebuild.

How can you build trust?

This is difficult to answer because building trust is not just one thing you can do, or say, to magically create trust with another person. But, there is a general rule you can follow—*do the right thing, no matter how great or small, even when no one is looking.* Of course, what makes this difficult is our own personal judgement of what's right and what's not. Yet, doing the right thing is what we should strive for every minute of the day. It's like having your own personal code of ethics.

Doing the right thing in a singular act is called being *honest.* When you do the right thing all the time, no matter how great or small, even when no one is looking, it's called *integrity.* Integrity comes from the heart. It's not a skill or tactic to develop, it's not a one-time thing, it's how you are. It's your personal rules, values, or morals you follow. Being honest and having integrity is something you do that helps build trust with others.

In *Lead the Field,* Earl Nightingale tells a story about an American general who was captured by the Chinese in the Korean War. The general was treated terribly and was subjected to brainwashing and intense interrogation. Yet, the general never caved. Finally, he was told that unless he answered their questions, he would be executed the next morning. Believing he would be put to death, he wrote a letter to his wife. At the end of the letter, he gave her a message to tell his son, "Tell Johnny the word is integrity." Thankfully, the general was not executed and was later returned to America. But of all the things the general could've told his son, in what he believed to be his last letter, he told him to be a person of integrity.

If you want to build trust, start with integrity—do the right thing all the time, even when no one is looking.

Another way to build trust with others is to do what you say you'll do, when you say you'll do it. People have certain expectations of you, as they do me. If we don't live up to their expectations, then the trust-level begins to break down. When the trust-level breaks down, they can't rely on us as they once could. If this happens and the trust is broken, we must work ten times as hard to repair it. Again, it all comes back to doing the right thing in the first place.

Closely related to "doing what you say you'll do, when you say you'll do it" is matching your actions to your words. In a relationship example, if someone says, "I love you," but their actions don't show it, do you believe their words? In a business example, sometimes a lofty mission statement or an aspiring culture is put into beautifully flowing words, yet the actions of the business say otherwise. How will the customers feel about this contradiction? How will the employees feel about working for a company that says one thing, but does another? How would you feel? It may go without saying, but this is a top-down problem that starts with the organization's leadership. Sure, it sounds great to say something aspiring, but you actually have to demonstrate it every day, to every one. Make sure your actions are consistent with your words.

And yet, one more way to build trust, in business and personal relationships, is to underpromise and overdeliver. It's natural to want to promise the moon. However, if you can't deliver the moon, then don't make the promise. Have you ever had a situation where you ordered something and you were told it would be here on a certain day? That certain day rolls around and you don't have your order. You wait a day or so, and still nothing. So you decide to call to find out what's going on. You get some type of excuse such as: it's on backorder, there's a materials shortage, the weather in another part of the country is delaying shipment, our systems are down, the vendor was waiting for more orders to justify the shipment, and so on. All of this may actually be true and a normal part of business. The problem with this is that the buyer makes plans around the expected delivery date. Whether those plans are actual plans or just in the mind, the expectation has been set. The only way to fix this in the future is to give the worst-case scenario for delivery. For example, let's say your products are delivered within one week 80 percent of the time, within two weeks 15 percent of the time, and within three weeks 5 percent of the time. Do you promise one week? How can you promise something that is not 100 percent? Let your customer know that it could take up to three weeks for delivery, however, it usually comes sooner. Write down the expected date three weeks from the order date; this will then be the date in which your customer fixates. If it comes in a week, yay, do the happy dance, you're the hero.

As we go through the remainder of this book, we'll look at other ways you can build trust. Trust starts with integrity, which starts with you. Trust is the relationship glue.

Exercise - Let's say one of your children makes a purchase of some candy with their own money. When you get home your child says, "Wow! Look Mommy, look Daddy, they gave me too much money back. It's like I got my candy for free!"

> ➤ What would you say to your child?
> ➤ If this situation happened to you, what would you do?

➤ If you led a team at work, what kind of person would you want on the team as it relates to this exercise?

➤ If you were on a team at work, whether or not you were the leader, and a similar situation happened with a client or a vendor, what would you do?

Questions for Growth

1. In a personal setting, has someone ever let you down?
2. How did this affect your level of trust for this person?
3. In a work setting, has someone ever let you down?
4. How did this affect your level of trust for this person?
5. Have you ever let someone down?
6. How did this affect your relationship with this person?
7. Are you a person who consistently does what you say you'll do, when you say you'll do it?
8. Even if you feel you're pretty good at doing what you say you'll do, how could you improve in this area?
9. Do you have a relationship that might need some repair work?
10. How does this apply to you in your work setting?

References and Sources:
o Dictionary.com
o Nightingale, Earl, *Lead the Field* (Nightingale-Conant

8

MINDSET

Your mindset is basically your way of thinking. It's your perspective—your way of looking at things. It's your attitude. And, it's your philosophy.

Much of the time, we all have a tendency to look at things from our own point of view—how it affects us. Don't feel bad, this is natural; we're human. But personal growth comes when we're able to look at things from the other person's point of view.

Let's look at a few situations to start the discussion of mindset, beginning with perspective.

Perspective—(outlook, point of view, way of looking at situations, position, angle)

Situation 1:

I once visited an advertising specialties store. An older man came out to greet me. After we exchanged pleasantries, he asked, "What kind of advertising items are you looking for?"

I said, "Well, I'm wanting one of those banner signs like speakers have on stage that shows the name or theme of their program."

The man replied, "You'll have to talk to my daughter about that. She's not here right now and I'm just filling in while she's gone. Here's a catalog you can take with you."

I took the catalog and said, "Okay, I'll look at the catalog and give her a call back later."

The man said, "Yes, give her a call. We need all the business we can get."

I turned around and walked out. But something about that last statement bothered me. I'm sure he didn't mean anything by it, but it kind of rubbed me the wrong way. So much so that I never went back.

Consider the statement, "We need all the business we can get." From whose perspective is this statement coming? What could this man have said differently?

Situation 2:

A friend of mine who is an accountant was complaining about a particular client. She said, "That man needs to realize I'm doing him the favor by doing his accounting work."

From whose perspective is this statement coming?

In your opinion, who is doing the favor, the accountant or the client?

Situation 3:

You're eating at a restaurant and your server brings you the check. You say, "Thank you." The server says, "You're welcome." When your server brings you the check, basically he or she is saying, "You can pay me now." And for some reason, we thank them for this opportunity to pay.

Or similarly, you're at a store paying for your items. The cashier hands you the receipt and you say, "Thank you." The cashier says, "You're welcome."

This situation is more subtle than the first two. First, why do we say thank you when someone hands us the bill or the receipt? Perhaps we're being polite? Why would the server or cashier say "You're welcome" in this situation? From whose perspective is this statement. What could the server or cashier say that would change it to the customer's perspective? Who should be doing the thanking?

Analysis

The purpose of the these three situations is to get you thinking about your perspective. These are very common examples that happen every day, and are considered normal. Most people don't even think about their perspective; they're just doing what feels natural—looking at things from their own point of view.

However, leaders on all stages of the ladder try to look at situations from the other person's perspective. Why? Leadership is not about you, it's about others—it's all about relationships. It's about serving and helping others. It's about being appreciative of others. If you want to connect more, start looking at things from the other person's perspective.

Attitude—(Your positive or negative view.)

As a teenager, I was a grass-cutting machine. My summers revolved around cutting grass. When I was 16 I probably had 30 to 40 lawns to mow, and I couldn't do it alone. My younger brother, Wes, would often help, but he was only 11. Back in those days we didn't mulch, we used a grass catcher on the side or in back of the mower. When the grass catcher was full, I'd dump it on an old bed sheet. My brother's job was to throw the bed sheet full of grass clippings over his shoulder and carry it to the trash pile. In the early 1980s, people paid $10 to $12 to have their lawn cut! So keep that paltry amount in mind as I tell you this next part.

For carrying the grass clippings to the trash pile, I paid my brother a nickel per bag. I know that sounds like I was cheap, and maybe I was. Well, on this one yard, Wes emptied 9 bags of grass clippings. His pay for emptying 9 bags at five cents per bag was 45 cents. After we finished mowing the lawn we went by the convenience store to get a Mountain Dew®. When Wes put his drink on the counter, the cashier said, "That'll be 50 cents."

Wes looked at me and I knew exactly what he was thinking. I said, "Do you want to borrow a nickel?"

I know you're thinking that I was a mean brother, I really wasn't. It was my job to make life difficult for my younger brother, that's what older brothers do. So, I loaned him the nickel.

That night at the dinner table, mom and dad asked how it went that day while we were cutting grass. Of course, Wes told them, in one breath, that he emptied 9 bags, earned a nickel per bag, received 45 cents, went to the convenience store to buy a Mountain Dew®, the Mountain Dew® cost 50 cents, and he had to borrow 5 cents from me to complete the purchase.

You would've thought I'd beat him up or something. My dad said, "You mean to tell me that he went to work for you today and rather than making money, he owes you a nickel?"

What could I say? That's how it happened.

Mom looked at my brother and asked, "Wes, how does that make you feel?"

Wes said, "It's okay, I was just glad I could get a Mountain Dew®."

Boy, did I feel like a heel.

As difficult as I had made it for my younger brother, he showed me what it means to have an attitude of gratitude.

For some reason, it's much easier to focus on the things that bother you. Negative stuff stands out because it's either painful, disruptive to our ideal plans, or because someone ticked you off. When something negative happens, it's obviously not part of the plan. But, negative stuff happens, that's just the way it is.

When positive things happen, or things go according to your ideal plan, you might not get too excited. Why not? Two reasons. One, you don't get excited because that's what you wanted, or expected, to happen. Two, when things go according to plan, it's not disruptive. If it's not disruptive, then you just keep going. It's easy to take positive things for granted, as if it was just supposed to happen that way, all the time.

When something negative happens, it's not uncommon for us to react.

You do it, I do it. We don't mean to, it just happens. But what actually causes us to react? Does another person cause you to react? Do certain people cause you to react more than others? Does bad weather on a day you have something planned outdoors cause you to react? What about a flat tire when you're in a hurry? What about when one of your children spills a drink (every time you go to a restaurant)? What is it specifically that causes you to react negatively (i.e., have a bad attitude)?

Well, the truth is, it's not the positive or negative people that determine your attitude. It's not the bad weather, the spilled drink, or the flat tire. It can't be these things because you don't have control over these things. However, there is one thing in all of these situations that you do have control over—it's you. You, and only you, decide how you will react to the situation. Think about it, how can a flat tire force you to have a bad attitude? It can't, it's just a tire. It's the same way with other people, they may know how to push your buttons, but only you can determine how you will react.

To grow as a leader, become aware of your attitude when something doesn't go your way. If you see yourself reacting, take a deep breath and do your best to remain calm. Think like a professional airline pilot—if something goes wrong, remain calm, fly the plane first, then handle the situation.

Strive for patience. Patience is not something you're born with, it's something you practice. Strive to keep your composure. Strive to remain calm when the situation gets rough. Practicing patience, composure, and calmness will help you develop a good attitude in spite of negativity. No, you don't have to get excited about the negative stuff, just handle it without all the drama.

A bad attitude creates a gap in your relationships—it pushes people away. A good attitude creates a connection in your relationships—people will respect you more when you have a good attitude. People will follow a person with a good attitude long before they'll follow someone with a bad attitude.

Philosophy—(reasoning process, principles, beliefs)

Your philosophy is how you interpret things based on your experiences and beliefs. You've inherited part of your parent's and sibling's philosophy. Teachers, friends, and even television have had an effect on your philosophy.

Everything that happens to you throughout the day is filtered through your philosophy. Your philosophy is not neutral; it either has a positive slant or a negative slant. How do you view the world? How do you view other people? How do you view your relationships? How do you view your job? How do you view your place in life? Are you pessimistic or optimistic?

Are you trusting or distrusting of others?

Most people don't think much about their philosophy or how they acquired it—it just is what it is. Have you thought much about your philosophy? What experiences led to your current philosophy? How does your philosophy affect your attitude? How does your philosophy affect your relationships?

Here's the big question—do you need a new or better philosophy?

To grow as a leader, take some time to consider your philosophy. What's your outlook on life? How do you think? How can you improve? What needs to change? Is there something in particular that's holding you back? Who can you talk to about improving your philosophy? What books can you read?

People are more likely to connect with someone who has a good, positive philosophy.

Questions for Growth

1. What experiences have influenced your thinking most?
2. What is your basic attitude toward life?
3. Who or what influenced your attitude most?
4. In general, what is your philosophy?
5. Is your view more inward-focused or outward-focused?
6. Is it possible to improve your mindset? If so, what improvements would you like to see?
7. What would you be willing to do to improve your mindset?
8. For at least one full day (or even half a day), will you look at each situation, good and bad, and try to find the positive, or at least try not to react?
9. In each situation ask, "What is it that's causing me to react?" If it's a tire, for example, ask, "How can a tire cause me to react? It's just a tire."

Recommended Reading:
o *A Life of Excellence: Wisdom for Effective Living* by Richard E. Simmons
o *My Philosophy for Successful Living* by Jim Rohn

9

ABILITY TO WORK WITH OTHERS

Life would be easy if it weren't for other people. Connie Podesta

Have you ever been frustrated with all the traffic while trying to get somewhere, without being late? It's like, your destination is not that far away, maybe just a few miles. How long does it take to drive a few miles, right? Like, five minutes? Oh heck no, it takes 30 minutes because of all the dadgum traffic. I recently had a similar situation trying to get my 10-year old son, Cole, to his baseball game. The game started at 5:30 p.m., but we had to be there by 5:00 p.m. for warm-ups. Even though it was a small town, folks were getting off work and the traffic was ridiculous. Cole could tell I was frustrated. He said, "Dad, if it weren't for all these people in our way, we might could get somewhere." He was right.

Have you ever felt that way, not necessarily in traffic, but maybe with the people you work with? Almost every workplace has that one person who is difficult. (If you don't think your workplace has a difficult person, it's possible that person might be you;-) Sometimes it's not just one person, it's everybody—they just seem to get on your last nerve. If these people weren't in your way you might be able to get somewhere! Does this sound familiar?

Unfortunately, or fortunately, depending on how you look at it, people are an inherent part of life. That's why it's called *life*. You must have people to have life. People are also an inherent part of your work life—co-workers, bosses, managers, customers, clients, vendors, consultants, and competitors. Everywhere you turn there are people, people, people.

After more (just a little more) than 50 years on earth, I'm beginning to think that we need people to make the world go round. Love 'em or hate 'em, there's no living without 'em.

Where we tend to drive ourselves crazy is when we think that *everyone* else needs to conform to our expectations. Sorry, but it ain't gonna happen, not on this planet. People were put here to rub you the wrong way! Not really, people are just different. And it's those differences that seem to give us the most trouble.

Have you ever tried to change someone? Why stop there, have you ever tried to change everyone you work with? Were you successful or frustrated? I'm betting on frustrated! And here's why. There's an age-old principle that's been around since the beginning of existence and it goes like this:

You can't change people.

I don't know why this is, but you just can't change people. It is impossible. Yet, so many of us try and try and try. I've tried, you've tried, we've all tried. Plain and simple, it just won't work.

However, before you move to a deserted island to get away from all those crazies you have to work with, there might be another way to deal with these ridiculous people.

Work with them. Yes, work *with* them. Consider this—if you're trying to change them you're actually working *against* them. That's what causes the friction. You might think it's the other person causing the friction, but it's probably not; it may be your working against them that's causing it. And your attempt to change someone is, and always will be, futile. It's futile because it goes against the age-old principle—you can't change people.

The people that seem to get ahead in life have figured this out. They realize that they can't change people, so they work with them. Your ability to work with others will actually help you succeed. It will make your life so much easier, you'll wonder why you didn't learn this on the playground in pre-K.

Yes, I know people can be difficult. I know it seems like their life purpose is to scratch their finger nails on your proverbial chalkboard. (*Note to Millennials*—A chalkboard is an obsolete device used in the classroom prior to dry-erase boards and electronic boards. It was usually a black or green board and you could write on it with chalk. Since chalkboards are no longer used in the classroom, chalk now comes in many colors and is used to draw on the sidewalk. However, if you ever see a chalkboard in an antique store, don't leave until you scratch your finger nails on it. This analogy will then make sense. Oh yeah, LOL.)

Yet, there is a purpose for all the difficulties and the differences with people. Can you imagine if we were all detail-oriented, analytical introverts? We'd all be accountants! (My apologies for stereotyping. But, stand by, I won't discriminate.) Or what if we were all talkative, joke-telling, back-slapping, life-of-the-party, out-going extroverts? We'd all be salespeople! (Just kidding, not all salespeople are extroverts.) Seriously, we need our differences to make the world go 'round. Different people are able to perform different jobs, and at different levels. Variety is mandatory for a properly functioning world, including your workplace.

Can you imagine a football team where everyone's a quarterback? Who would snap the ball? Who would block the other team? Who would run the ball? Who would catch a pass? Who would kick and who would punt? Who would play defense?

Thankfully, we're all different! We need one another to make this whole thing, called life, work.

So what do we need to do? The principle, *you can't change people,* is not entirely true. Even though you may not be able to change other people, there is one person you can change—you.

If people get in your way, get under your skin, and drive you crazy, perhaps it's time to change your mindset toward others. No, it's not easy. But, at least it is possible. Changing others is impossible; changing yourself is possible. Why is it possible? Changing yourself is possible because you're the one in control—you can't control others, but you can control yourself.

Once you decide that changing others is impossible and you decide to try something different, one of the best places to start is with your people-view. Your people-view is just that, how you view others. If you view people as a mass (a collection of incoherent particles forming one body), then you will not have much care for the individuals that make up the mass. On the other hand, if you see people as individual persons, you will begin to care for their well-being. Oh, and just so you'll know, people are not masses, they really are individual persons.

When you see people as individual persons, you'll realize that each person has an individual personality. Each person has a heart. And just like you and me, they have needs, wants, desires, problems, and bless their heart, they have in-laws (for this reason alone you've got to give them some slack)!

People are individual persons, just like you are a person. In some weird sort of mixed up way, we're all special. For some people you may have to look really close, and I do mean really close, but there's something special there (I'm almost sure of it).

Have you ever sat in the middle of the mall and just watched all the different people walk by? Of course, it's an acceptable thing in society to "people watch." People watching is not staring, at least, not until they pass by, right? Then, you stare at them wondering why they came out in public looking that way. What in the world were they thinking? And then you think, "Whew, I'm shore glad I ain't that person."

Okay, just so you'll know, when you make or think these critical remarks about someone, it's called judging. Yes, even though you didn't say it out loud, it's still judging.

We judge people based on where *we* come from, not where *they* come from. Yet, we have no idea where they're coming from. We don't know what they've been through, how they were raised, nor their financial condition. There's no way to know how you would be today if you had been in their situation all your life.

The next time you go to the mall to people watch, try a different angle. Rather than judging them based on how they look on the outside, look at them as a person and consider what's on the inside. Try to imagine where that person is coming from. Imagine what they've been through and how they were raised. Imagine their financial condition. Is it possible to view this person with kindness and compassion rather than indifference and judgement? I'm not trying to get all mushy here, I'm just trying to drive home the point that people are individual persons, just like you and me. Everyone's situation is different, and for the most part, no one can control the environment in which they were raised.

Now, after doing this little experiment at the mall, try it at work. Look at the people you work with as individual persons. You don't have to be their best friend, just have some kindness and compassion for them. This people-as-persons perspective will make it much easier for you to work with them, rather than against them. Look for a connection rather than a rejection.

Your ability to work with others will improve your ability to connect. No, things won't always be perfect, but your ability to work with others will help you navigate through stressful situations. Of course it's easy to work well with others when everything is going smoothly (i.e., going your way). The real test comes when the road gets bumpy—project deadlines, stress, hurt feelings, breakdowns, shortages, etc.

In the coming chapters we will look at specific skills to improve your ability to work with others. For now, the evidence that you work well with others is shown by your:
- Ability to listen
- Approachability
- Calmness in times of stress
- Communication skills
- Concern for others
- Encouragement of others
- Flexibility
- Helping others
- Patience
- Respect of others
- Setting an example for others

These are just a few traits that demonstrate how well you work with others. How do you rank on each one? Are there obvious areas where you need to improve? Are there areas where you feel you are strong? The idea behind self-improvement is to build on strengths and work on your relevant weaknesses[1]. It's impossible for any one person to score a perfect ten in all areas. But, the more you improve, even small improvements, the better you'll connect with others.

[1] Relevant weaknesses are weaknesses that relate to your pursuit of success. If you have a weakness that does not relate, then don't spend much time trying to improve it. Focus on your strengths and the weaknesses that are important components to your growth.

Questions for Growth

1. Describe someone, without naming names, who grates on your nerves.
2. Is it possible that you grate on the nerves of others?
3. Have you ever tried to change someone else? How'd it go?
4. Is it difficult to see others as individuals, with their own needs, wants, desires, and problems?
5. On a scale of 1 to 10 (lowest to highest), how would you rate your flexibility to work with others?
6. Do you have room for improvement when it comes to working with others?
7. What do you like about your job? Make a list of anything and everything that you like. Every day, read your list and try to add to it. The purpose is to focus on the positive aspects of your work, and to minimize the negative.

10

WHAT PEOPLE WANT

There's one thing people want more than anything else. And all the leadership skills you learn should help you give people this one thing they desire most. What is this one thing?

More than anything else people want to be *understood*.

Have you ever talked to someone who tends to rebut everything you say? They tell you why you shouldn't feel the way you do; they try to fix it, when you really just want them to listen; they top it with something bigger that has happened to them; or maybe they interrupt you while you're trying to finish a thought. Do you feel like they were really listening? Do you feel heard? Do you feel understood? Most likely not. Listening, or lack of listening, in this manner creates an unfulfilled gap.

Sometimes you just want someone to listen—no rebuttal, no fixing it, no topping it, and no interrupting—just listening. And when you find that person who will listen, it's like a weight has been lifted off your chest. You feel better just having expressed what's on your mind. What a great feeling!

It's rare to find this person who will just listen. It could be a friend, spouse, or co-worker. It may even be a therapist. In fact, if you have a friend, spouse, or co-worker who will actually listen, it's like having your own therapist—the relief you have when someone listens is therapeutic to your soul!

This type of listening is more than just listening, otherwise you could talk to your dog or cat. (Your dog or cat may look like they're listening, but they're just lying there bored out of their tiny little minds; that's why they sleep all the time!) The real listening that gives you relief is when someone listens to understand. They sincerely want to hear you, they care about what you're saying, and they want to know *why* this is important to you. You have their undivided attention allowing you to say what's on your mind.

Where the first type of listening described above creates a gap (seems like it makes things worse), listening to understand creates a connection by filling the gap. If you want to create more connections, start listening—really listening. Don't worry about fixing it, don't give unsolicited advice, don't top it with something bigger, and don't interrupt. Just listen to understand. Give them your undivided attention. Put down your phone and don't look at your computer. Ask clarifying questions to make sure you're on the same page. By the end of the conversation, you should know where they're coming from and why.

Listening to understand is not an easy feat. It can actually be quite painful at first. You may feel like you're about to explode to blurt out something that will fix the whole thing, but don't, just don't. You may also find that you disagree or do not share the same views. That's okay, you don't have to start a debate about who's right or wrong. Let your views go and just listen to understand—that's it, plain and simple, right?

Well, no, it's not all that plain and simple. Listening to understand takes practice. You can practice on your friends, spouse, kids, co-workers, or even a random stranger who happens to need an ear. My wife and kids provide me with plenty of opportunity to practice, everyday! Practicing on those who are close to you is actually more difficult than practicing on a stranger. We are more comfortable with our family members and we have a vested interested in their lives. With a stranger, not so much.

To truly understand what someone is saying you must hear more than words. Listen for the meaning behind the words. Ask relevant questions to help you better understand. Every now and then, paraphrase what you've heard and how it's making them feel. It's okay to ask if there's anything you can do to help, but leave it at that. Resist the urge to provide unsolicited advice, unless, of course, it is solicited.

If you truly want to connect with others, listen to understand.

In the next chapter we'll dig deeper into developing your listening skills.

Questions for Growth

1. Do you consider yourself a good listener, or is it painful?
2. Do you ever feel like someone is not really listening to you; they tell you that you shouldn't feel that way, they try to fix it, or they top it with something bigger?
3. If you answered "yes" to question 2, how does that make you feel?
4. Is it possible you do the same to others?
5. Do you feel the need to "fix it" when others talk?
6. Do you feel the need to offer advice, even if it's not requested?
7. Do you have room to improve your listening to understand skills?
8. Where could you start?

11

HOW TO LISTEN

In the previous chapter we talked about what people want—to be understood. For you to understand them, you must be a good listener. In this chapter we'll discuss a few of the ways you can improve your listening skills starting today. Heck, why don't we start right now?

> ➤ Face the person who is talking. If you don't face the person who is talking, but only turn your head, your body language is saying, "I wish you'd hurry because you interrupted something that's more important to me." Turn your chair, turn your shoulders, and turn your body. Square your shoulders to the other person. When you face the person who is talking you're saying, "You, and what you have to say, are important to me."

> ➤ Make eye contact. Look at the other person; look at their facial expressions; and look at what their eyes are saying. Remember the metaphor, "the eyes are a window to the soul." You can really tell a lot about what someone is thinking and feeling when you look into their eyes.

> ➤ Be attentive. This refers to your physical attention. Remove your distractions. Put down your phone, don't look at your computer, and turn off the television. Focus your attention on the person who is talking.

> ➤ Be present. This refers to your mental attention. Clear your mind of distractions. If there's something on your mind, either write it down or ask if you can have just a minute to finish up.

> ➤ Schedule time to listen. If you're just too busy at the moment or you're facing a deadline, ask if you can schedule some time a little later. Also, explain why you can't take the time right now. Make sure you communicate your willingness to listen and that you want to provide your full attention.

- ➢ Ask relevant questions. When you ask questions that relate to what the other person is saying, they know you're listening.
- ➢ Ask clarifying questions. Ask questions to make sure you're getting it.
- ➢ Don't look for opportunities to talk. The average listener can't listen because they're too busy looking for an opportunity to talk. Above average listeners resist the urge to talk. Make a mental note or jot down a one word reminder. The point is to focus on the other person. Save *your* drama for another time.
- ➢ Don't listen from your perspective. Often, people listen with only one question in mind—how does this affect me? Resist this urge and listen to the whole thing first. Later, you can determine how it affects you.
- ➢ Don't interrupt!
- ➢ Respect that there may be a difference in opinion. When someone talks, you're not always going to have the same opinion. Your views, morals, or philosophy may be different. That's okay, you don't have to start a debate or fix the other person's way of thinking to agree with yours. Resist judgement.
- ➢ Care about the other person, about what's being said, and why it's important to them.
- ➢ Keep it to yourself. Maintain confidence of the entire conversation, and the fact that the conversation even occurred. Whatever you do, don't share what you've heard with anyone else—that's a quick way to destroy trust.
- ➢ Don't offer unsolicited advice like, "You just need to…" Rather, let them know you'd be willing to help if possible, such as, "Is there anything I can do to help?"

In short, listening creates connections because real, genuine, authentic listening draws people closer to you. However, most people are not that good at listening. If you just learn the skill of active listening, you can easily be ahead of most people.

According to author Robert Bolton, Ph.D., in his book, *People Skills*, "Eighty percent of the people who fail at work do so for one reason: they do not relate well to other people." He also writes, "There is one thing certain about your methods and style of communication: they are primarily learned responses."

Knowing that listening is such an important part of communication and one's success, and that it is a learned skill, why aren't more people better listeners? Simple: it requires work. If it was that easy, everyone would be doing it and the world would be full of peace and love. To improve your listening skills, you must first desire to improve, then start practicing. No, it's not easy, but the rewards are well worth the disciplined effort. The more you do it, the better you'll become.

Good leaders are good listeners. Listening, real listening, creates connections.

Questions for Growth

1. Do you consider yourself a good listener? Why or why not?
2. How do you feel when someone "unloads" on you?
3. How do you feel when someone wants to talk, but you're extremely busy at the moment?
4. If someone is talking to you about something in which you have a different opinion, or a different moral, religious, or political view, what do you do? How does this affect your listening ability?
5. Do you have a tendency to interrupt before the other person has finished?
6. Do you have a desire to fix the situation?
7. Do you offer your advice, even though it may not have been requested?
8. Are you able to maintain complete confidence about the conversation and the fact that the conversation happened?

References and Sources:

Bolton Ph.D, Robert, *People Skills: How to Assert Yourself, Listen to Others, and Resolve Conflicts* (Simon & Schuster, Inc, 1986), 7, 8

12

MAJOR ROAD BLOCK

When it comes to connecting with people, there's one thing that creates a major road block—*pride*.

In simple terms, pride is placing yourself higher than another person. Pride is the opposite of humbleness—being humble means placing yourself lower than another person. On a scale of 1 to 10, humbleness is a 1 and pride is a 10. Think of pride as a road block that prevents passage. If there is no passage, then there is no connection. Here are a few problems caused by pride.

➤ Pride blocks you from admitting when you are wrong, even when it's blatantly obvious. There is always some reason to justify why you did or said something. To a person with pride, even the smallest things are more important than the other person. If you have pride, it's more important for you to be right than to admit you're wrong.

➤ Pride blocks you from giving a sincere, heartfelt apology. You may voice some form of an apology, but typically it's just words that don't feel genuine. Many times the apology comes after the other person has had to explain 19-ways-to-Sunday why you were wrong and why it hurt their feelings, yet, you keep defending yourself. And then, maybe, you finally say, "Well I'm *sorry.*" (Note the emphasis wasn't on *I'm.*) And even if it were heartfelt, an apology received after working so hard to explain the problem is hardly fulfilling nor worth the effort. The worst resemblance of an apology is "I'm sorry *you* feel that way." You're better off not giving this type of non-apology at all. You're not actually saying you are sorry, you're basically telling the other person they shouldn't feel the way they do.

➤ Pride blocks you from seeing the other person's perspective. If you

51

only look at things from your perspective, nothing else, or no one else, will ever be as important as you are.

When you have pride, you're unwilling to let the other person be higher than you, not in terms of a position at work, but in terms of vulnerability. For example, a sincere, heartfelt apology would put the other person higher than you because you would be admitting guilt. If you were to admit guilt, you may feel you're placing yourself beneath the other person. This makes you feel vulnerable, like you're lowering your guard. The only reason for keeping up your guard is to protect your pride. It's not like you'll be physically bruised; pride is only in your mind. Being unwilling to be humble to another person, even when it's obvious that you should be, creates a divide in your relationships. And each time this happens, and it goes unresolved, without a heartfelt, sincere reconciliation, then a layer of resentment builds. Resentment doesn't happen by choice, it happens automatically, often unknowingly, one layer at a time, until there's a wall of resentment that is too high to tear down. Whatever you do, don't leave unresolved conflict; always reconcile.

Pride is a form of defensiveness. Defensiveness causes you to react too quickly to even consider the situation. When I first started working in public accounting I remember having a desk in the staff bullpen, a large room of about 24 cubicles. When sitting at a cubicle, I couldn't see much, but I could hear practically everything. On one occasion the office manager, a very sweet lady, came to the bullpen, walked over to John's (not his real name) desk and asked if he would move his car so a delivery truck could get by. Her tone was very kind and non-accusatory. John immediately responded, "My car's not in the way." The office manager seemed a little surprised and kindly said, "Well, the truck driver is concerned and really just wants to take precautions." John quickly rebutted, "What kind of driver is he? Maybe he needs to take some driving lessons."

John eventually moved his car, but there was no way he was going to admit it was necessary to do so. In his mind, it was the same as admitting he was wrong. Nobody said he was wrong about anything, yet he felt accused. The problem, though, was caused by John and where he chose to park his car. Rather than parking in the staff parking like everyone else, he chose to park on the outer edge of the parking lot on the grass. This spot happened to be about 50 steps closer to the building than the staff parking lot.

Defensiveness is a guard against perceived criticism and a protection of our ego. Perhaps John felt he was being criticized for where he chose to park. He definitely knew that he should be parking in the parking lot and not on the grass. What if everyone decided to park on the grass? Whether John was right or wrong, it sure did appear to hurt his ego.

As a side note, John actually had a hard time connecting with his coworkers. He seemed to know everything and was always right, in his mind. He didn't last long at the firm.

If you truly want to connect with someone, it is of utmost importance to the relationship to remove any road block of pride—your pride. Now, if you're thinking about removing someone else's pride you're probably not thinking about this from the right angle. We're talking about *your* pride. You can't change other people. You can try and try until you're blue in the face, yet someone with pride will only defend it.

Pride is such a road block that, most of the time, someone with pride can't even see that they are full of pride. Even when you tell them they are being prideful, they get defensive. Before you can remove pride, you must become aware of it, at least to the *possibility* that you may have pride. Then, as difficult as this may seem, find someone you can talk to about it. Obviously, this person needs to be someone you trust, so that you will have no need to feel defensive. In situations like this where privacy is important, it is often a good idea to talk with a mentor or coach.

The bottom line, connections are created through open communication. The fewer road blocks to open communication, the better, deeper, and easier the connection. And of course, the better the relationships.

Questions for Growth

1. Has anyone ever told you that you are prideful?
2. Do you think you are prideful? Why or why not?
3. How easy, or difficult, is it for you to give a heartfelt, sincere apology?
4. Are you quick to apologize, or does the other person have to explain it to you (sometimes over and over)?
5. Would you consider yourself a defensive person?
6. How important is it for you to be right in most situations?
7. How do you leave a conflict? Do you just stop talking about it after both of you are exhausted, or do you have a genuine reconciliation?
8. How do you feel about other people's feelings?

13

BE APPROACHABLE

In the previous chapters we've talked about communication:
- ➤ What people want—to be understood
- ➤ How to listen
- ➤ Road blocks that prevent open communication (pride and defensiveness)

Now what?

Now it's time to be approachable.

Have you ever noticed there are some people who always seem to be smiling, and then there are others with a permanent scowl? Which person is more approachable? I hope you said the smiling person. So let's start here—look in the mirror. Which person are you? The first thing you can do if you want to be more approachable is—wipe that scowl off your face and start smiling. It is that simple.

Second, advertise your open door policy. What, you say you don't have an open door policy? Then, start now. You know that person who always has their office door closed? Do you knock? Do you try to catch them when they take a bathroom break? Do you email? What do you do? You hate to bother them. Get the point? If you don't like that, then don't do that to others. If you want to be a leader who connects with people, stop isolating yourself in your ivory tower and open your door. You don't have to be available 24/7; just be available periodically. Yes, you're going to have appointments and you need to get work done—I get it. Let those around you know when you are available. Literally give them a schedule. When it's their turn, give them your undivided attention. Don't change it, don't avoid them, and don't keep looking at your watch.

Third, communicate that you are willing to help. Don't be too busy to help. Leaders help people. If you want to connect with people you must be willing to help them.

Fourth, listen more than you talk. You know that person who talks all the time—primarily about themselves, of course. They talk about last night's game, what somebody should've or shouldn't have done, politics (as if they're the expert), their kids, their dog, and everything else they're interested in or have an opinion about. And it's the details—more details than an Ernest Hemingway novel. Or, what about the person who calls you to talk. You see their number on the caller ID, and you hesitate. You're thinking, "I don't have an hour to listen to all the details of the latest drama." They're the kind of person who just can't talk for five to ten minutes; it's an hour or more! Even though I've exaggerated this a bit, do you get how annoying this is? Don't be that person. Leaders listen. Listen more than you talk.

Fifth, be genuinely concerned about others. Show that you care. Ask them how things are going. Ask about their family. Ask for their opinion or insight. This is not the same as asking, "Hey, how's it going?" as you continue walking. Stop, sit down, and be concerned about what's really going on. Want to connect with people? Demonstrate your genuine concern.

The basic idea of being an approachable leader is to have a welcoming persona. It's who you are. You speak to people, you listen, and you care. And that leads us to the next topic—caring.

Questions for Growth

1. Do you consider yourself approachable? Provide an example or two.
2. Are you a scowler or a smiler?
3. Do you make time for your co-workers who rely on you for assistance?
4. When you do make time, is it your undivided attention, or are you in a hurry?
5. How would you rank your talk/listen ratio? For example, 70/30 means you talk 70 percent of the time and listen 30 percent of the time.
6. How would you describe your concern for others? Do you ask how they're doing, with the intent of actually wanting to know?

14

CARING

Leaders care.

Generally, there are two things leaders care about. First, leaders care about others. Second, they care about the work they've chosen to pursue.

Caring about others

How can you influence people through your leadership if you don't genuinely care about them? Leadership influence is not about getting your way, it's about helping others get their way. Sure, you may want to climb the corporate ladder or build a successful business of your own, but you can't do it without helping or serving others. Zig Ziglar said, "You can get everything in life you want, if you will just help enough other people get want they want." To get what you want, you must put others first.

Caring is about being kind and compassionate. Caring is showing concern for the well-being of others. Some people equate a leader with a stern, determined, and success-minded person who will stop at nothing and step over anyone to win. Yes, leaders tend to pursue success, but it doesn't mean a leader can't be kind and compassionate as well. Leaders don't have to be jerks—unless they want to push people away.

If you want to connect with people be kind, be compassionate, and be caring.

Caring about the work you've chosen to pursue

If you don't give a hoot about what you do, then do something else. How can you be excellent at something that you don't really care about? Do you like what you do? Is this just a job? Is there something else you'd like better? You've got to decide what it is you care about it, and then go after it.

Here's the problem when you don't care about what you do—it shows.

It shows in your performance, it shows in your attitude, and it shows on your face.

This isn't about following your passion or doing what you love (and the money will somehow magically follow). I mean, are accountants really passionate about debits and credits? Are they balancing books because they love it? No! However, they do care about professionalism and they care about the people they serve. They also care about their fellow accountants. Show me an accountant who cares and I'll show you an excellent accountant.

If you don't care about what you do, how can you influence others to care about what they do? What you do is important to someone—your employer, your customers/clients, and perhaps others who benefit (in the case of accountants, the IRS benefits from accurate reporting).

Good leaders care about those around them and they care about the work they've chosen to pursue.

In some cases the caring trait may come naturally from *within* the leader. They have a built-in desire to help and serve others. This inherent desire guides the leader through life. Caring and serving others comes first, the job or position comes second. In fact, their work may very well be chosen based on the desire to serve others (teachers, pastors, charitable, etc.).

Caring may also come from *outside* the leader in the form of responsibility. From this angle, taking care of the needs of followers is what's expected as part of the job or position. Who are the followers? Followers may include customers, clients, employees, co-workers, vendors, shareholders, the public, and anyone else somehow connected to the business. These leaders choose the job/position/career first. To rise as a leader in their work, caring about others is just part of the responsibility. This form of caring happens most frequently in business settings.

Neither form (or source) of caring is more or less important. It doesn't matter if the caring comes naturally from within or if the caring is part of the leader's responsibility; neither is better or worse than the other. Some people are led by caring first, and will do whatever job fulfills their desire to serve. Others will seek a career first, and serve others as part of the work. Whether caring comes from within the person or as part of the work's responsibility, the important thing is that people are the most important factor to the success of either.

Caring builds connections. When someone feels that you genuinely care, they will be drawn to you. Often, it is you, the leader, who breaks the ice to get a relationship started. You show interest in someone, they see you care, then they respond. And so the connection is made. However, this is not a one-time thing. To build and continue the relationship, you must continue the process of caring and interacting with others.

How do you show you care? To show you care, focus on the needs of others. It doesn't have to be something big all the time. The little things count significantly. Start by listening to those around you. What's on their mind? What insights can they share? What are their concerns? You don't necessarily have to solve every problem you hear, in fact, you may not even be able to. Many times someone just wants to talk and needs someone (who actually cares) to listen.

Leaders care about others and they care about the work they've chosen to pursue.

Questions for Growth

1. What is your situation with regard to your source of caring? Are you in a certain job, such as public service, because you have an inherent desire to serve? Or. are you in a job where you chose the career, and caring is part of the responsibility?
2. How did you get into the work you're currently doing?
3. Do you care about what you do, or is it just a job?
4. How do you demonstrate your care for others?
5. Have you ever performed a small act of kindness for someone, without expecting anything in return?
6. Can you think of someone who needs to know that you care?
7. Can you think of someone who needs for you to listen?
8. Is there some other line of work, or another position, you'd rather be doing?

15

GROWING AS A LEADER

There are differing opinions about whether you are born a leader or you learn to be a leader. I do believe some people are born with certain traits that lend themselves to being a leader. Confidence is a good example—some people are naturally more confident than others. However, I'm from the school of leadership-can-be-learned and I believe anyone who wants to be a leader can be a leader. And, anyone who is a leader can improve as a leader.

Let's start with your current work. Leadership can always be improved within your current role. By increasing your leadership competence, you will increase your effectiveness. How? Here are a few ideas to get you started.

➢ Do your job with excellence.

➢ Learn all you can about your current work. Look for opportunities to expand your knowledge and skills.

➢ Observe how your work serves others. Whom do you serve? How can you serve them better? Make it your priority to serve with excellence.

➢ Train others. Create a system of processes and procedures. A system is not a set of rules, it's a guide. With written systems, training time and costs are reduced in the long-run (see chapter 28).

➢ Maintain a positive and optimistic attitude about your job, the people you serve, those you work with, and yourself.

➢ Be a good listener rather than a talker. Listening is the only way to learn. What is there to learn? You'll learn about problems, issues, and concerns from the people you serve and the people on your team. Ask questions to help uncover these issues before they become major problems. Often, people won't say anything until the problem blows up.

➢ Be a problem solver. Problems happen, that's life. Rather than groan and complain, look for solutions. Solicit input from the people on your team and from your customers. Be open to any and all ideas.

➤ Work with others, not against them. Be flexible. That doesn't mean you have to give in to everyone else. It means to at least consider the ideas of others. If you're constantly shutting people down, they'll eventually stop talking to you altogether. It also means that your routines may be interrupted from time to time—just roll with it.

➤ Develop your people skills. Your people skills covers a broad spectrum. People skills relate to how well you listen, communicate, and interact with others.

➤ Set an example. Basically, people look for guidance from those around them. If you're in a leadership role, then lead by example. If you want people to dress a certain way, then you set the example. If you want people to be on time, then you be on time. Whatever you do will be mimicked by those around you.

As you can see from this list, there's much more to having a job than just going to work, doing your job, and going home. Yes, doing the minimum job requirements may suffice for a while, but eventually will be revealed. Think of your work capacity on a scale of 1 to 10. Doing the minimum is a 1. Performing your work with excellence is a 10. Where do you feel that you fit on the scale? Where would others say you fit? Why perform at the minimum (or close to the minimum) when there's so much more capacity that can lead to much more potential? As an added benefit, growing as a leader increases your effective performance, not only in your work life, but also in your personal life.

What about leadership growth opportunities outside of work? Perhaps you can serve at a charitable organization or your church. These organizations are always looking for volunteers and they provide an excellent opportunity for you to practice your leadership skills.

Have you considered joining a service club such as Rotary, Kiwanis, Sertoma, Lions Club, or Exchange Club? You won't be in the club long at all before you're being asked to serve. That doesn't have to be a bad thing. Consider it an opportunity for growth. In fact, rather than waiting to be asked to serve, be proactive about serving. Someone in the club is in charge of service opportunities. Sit down with this club member and learn all you can. In particular, look for something that interests you most, then jump in and get to work. After you've been in the club for a while, look for opportunities to hold a position (and there are plenty to choose from!). Keep moving up the position ladder and you'll eventually become club president!

You can also grow as a leader by reading and studying; and not just leadership topics, but anything that will help you in your work and your service to others. What do you need to learn? What do you want to learn? Whatever it is, there's a book to teach you.

Growing as a leader involves helping others to grow as well. This doesn't mean to go out and start telling people what to do and how to do it. In fact, many people don't want to know any more than is necessary to do their job with minimum effort. However, there are a few people who want more out of life and their work. Look for these people who have a desire to learn, and then help them. Share your knowledge, share your experience, and share your philosophy of serving others.

Growing as a leader starts with your desire to grow. There are plenty of opportunities to grow if you're open. When it comes to your personal development, you're either growing or shrinking—there is no status quo. Put another way, you're either moving forward or backward—there is no standing still. If you stand still, don't be surprised if someone passes you. When do we stop growing? We stop growing when we get comfortable. Maybe we should make ourselves uncomfortable on purpose. Keep moving, keep growing, and keep learning.

Lastly, growing as a leader means developing and strengthening relationships. Remember, leadership is all about relationships. Be interested in people, show you care, and serve them. This is the sure-fire recipe for making connections. It's really not about you, it's about others. And the more you focus on others, the more you'll grow as a person and a leader.

Questions for Growth

1. Do you feel that you were born with some leadership traits? Describe.
2. What leadership areas would you like to develop further?
3. How would you describe the way you perform your work on a scale of 1 to 10, with 1 being minimum effort and 10 being excellence?
4. Do you currently, or have you ever, volunteered for a non-profit organization?
5. Do you currently, or have you ever, been a member of a service club? If so, what positions did you hold?
6. Do you feel like you're moving forward, going backward, or standing still?
7. Do you desire to grow?
8. What have you done to pursue growth?
9. What course of action would you be willing to pursue?

16

IMPORTANCE OF CONTACTS

If leadership is about relationships and relationships are about people, then people must be about connections. In other words, you must first connect with people to have a relationship in order to have influence or impact as a leader. So how do you connect with people? Here's an example that you can implement today.

In the late 1990s, I asked some friends in my service club if anyone knew of a good place to stay at the beach. Sure enough, someone gave me the name of a lady who owned a condo in Panama City Beach, Florida. So I called her.

She says, "Yes, the condo is right on the beach, fourth-floor with gulf view, and it's $75 a night. So that would be $150 for the weekend."

"Okay, that sounds pretty good," I said, "but what about the tax and cleaning fee?"

"Mr. Sadler, it's all included."

"Really? Other places charge $125 or more, plus a cleaning fee. How in the world can you rent it for only $75 a night?"

She says, "I use word-of-mouth, rather than a management company—so I don't have to pay all those fees."

I was like, "Okay then, I'll take it!"

The condo was awesome and I stayed there two years in a row—same price, $75 a night.

Then, over the next couple of years, I started my own business, sold my house, moved to an apartment, bought another house—and by the time I was ready to go back to the beach, I couldn't find the lady's number anywhere.

I went back to the guy who I thought had told me about the condo, but he had no idea what I was talking about. I couldn't even recall this lady's name to look her up in the phone book (yes, we had phone books back then). So you know what happened? Absolutely nothing—I never stayed there again.

What was the problem?

Was it my fault because I didn't keep up with her phone number? Partially. However, in business, if your customer can't find you, it's definitely not their fault—it's yours! The problem was—*she* didn't keep in touch. A simple postcard each year with her contact information would've worked. Rather, she left it up to me to keep in touch with her. Her goal was keeping her costs down, not building repeat customers.

What's the point? You must nurture your relationships. The best way to do that is simply to keep in touch. And how can you keep in touch unless you maintain some form of contacts database? It doesn't matter if you maintain your contacts in a CRM (contact relationship management) software, on your phone, or in a written address book. The database form is not important; keeping in touch is extremely important.

Building and maintaining your contacts is an integral part of relationship building. Keeping in touch is the stuff that builds familiarity and trust. Think of your address book as your network of connections. Some people call it your sphere of influence. Do you have a small sphere or a large sphere? To build your sphere, make it your objective to meet people on a daily basis. Get their business card and add them to your database. Send them an email or a handwritten note and say, "Hey _____, it was great meeting you yesterday. Thank you for the info about the _____. I really appreciate it. Your name." Just a simple, cheesy little note; but it helps people remember you.

You never know how one connection can make a difference—in your life or someone else's life. Let's say you're considering applying for a certain job and you recall someone in your contacts who works there. Reach out to them to get their insight about the job and the company. Ask relevant questions and be appreciative for the help. Don't ask for them to pull any strings on your behalf, simply ask, "If you were me, what would you do to improve your chances of getting this position?" Then listen.

What if this scenario was turned around and you had the chance to help one of your contacts? Would you be willing to help? Could you make a difference in their life?

Think about these two scenarios—what level of help would you, or the other person, be willing to provide? Obviously, it depends on the strength of your relationship. Do you have a strong connection or a weak connection? Have you kept in touch? Have you been a giver or a taker in the relationship? Whatever you do, don't be the kind of person who only comes around when you need something. Call someone, or stop by to see them, and say, "Hey, I just wanted to check in on you and see how you're doing." If you're sincere and you don't have any other agenda, it'll blow them away.

Let me tell you about this one friend of mine who really made an impression on me. Backstory: We bought a house in Florida and on the day of closing we found out the sellers were from our hometown—small world, right? Up to this point I still hadn't actually met them. So within a few weeks after closing I decided to reach out to introduce myself. The guy's name is Brantlee Lawrence. After talking and texting a couple of times, I felt that he was a genuinely nice guy. Over the next few months we continued talking periodically. When I found out that he was in the insurance business, I asked if he could help with my auto insurance. He did. After that, I asked if I could move my homeowner's insurance to him. He did. Well, during this process he called to check on me and to see if I had any questions. When he called I happened to be unloading a trailer full of furniture at our new house. Brantlee asked, "Can I come by and give you a hand?" Of course I said no, but I really appreciated the offer. After we hung up the phone, I didn't think anything else about it. Until, 15 minutes later, Brantlee shows up with his sleeves rolled up to help me finish unloading the trailer. (Did I mention it was 95 degrees and humid?) And that's just the kind of guy he is.

Leaders build a network of connections. If you want to grow as a leader and make more connections, then build and maintain your contacts. If you want to build stronger connections, then keep in touch and be a giver.

Questions for Growth

1. Do you maintain a list of contacts?
2. If not, why not?
3. If you do maintain a list of contacts, do you keep in touch?
4. How do you go about growing your contacts list?
5. What do you do to strengthen your relationships?
6. Have you ever had someone get in touch with you just to see how you're doing? If so, how did it make you feel?
7. Could you make it a habit to contact one person per day for no other reason but to see how they're doing?

17

YOUR FOLLOWING

Many business people don't think of themselves as leaders; they think of themselves as business owners. Yet, business people are leaders. If you are a business owner, not only do you lead the people who work for your business, but you also lead the people who support your business—that is, your following. Consider the following actual scenario (names have been changed to protect the innocent).

Bob is in the tree removal business. I hired Bob to remove some pine trees at my home. As his crew was finishing the job, Bob and I stood in my front yard talking. He said, "Yeah, one of your neighbors down the street came by and asked me to give him a quote and he acted like he didn't even know me, when I had cut down some trees for him a few years back. When I reminded him, he acted like he didn't even know who I was. Then, he ends up getting somebody else to do the job. I just don't get it."

I asked, "How long ago has it been since you did the tree job for him?"

Bob thought for a moment, "Oh I don't know, maybe five to ten years ago."

I said, "Bob, I'm just curious, have you had any contact with him in the past five to ten years?"

"Well, no, like what do you mean?" Bob replied, not having a clue what I was suggesting.

Okay, let's stop this conversation right here. My neighbor, who requested the quote from Bob, obviously was not one of Bob's loyal followers. And Bob just couldn't understand it. Bob's feelings and his pride were hurt. He'd done some work for my neighbor in the past, so why in the world didn't the neighbor at least remember Bob?

Do you want the short answer? Bob didn't even try to build an ongoing relationship with my neighbor. And come to think of it, he hasn't with me either.

Many business and salespeople are similar to Bob—they do business with someone once, and that's it. If the customer happens to come back later, then great. If they don't come back, then "Oh well," or in the words of Doris Day, "Que sera, sera."

Is Bob a leader to his customers? Not by a long shot. Bob has little influence and has made little impact on his past customers. Don't get me wrong, Bob is a nice guy; he's just not an effective leader for the people he serves. Unfortunately, this example is all too common.

As business owners we must change our mindset from making sales to building relationships. A sale is not the end, it's the beginning. A sale is simply an introduction to a long-term business relationship, which may or may not become part of your following.

What exactly is a Following?

Here are a few examples:
- ➢ Whom does a school serve? Its students.
- ➢ Whom does a church serve? Its congregation. (Some say the community. Rather, the church serves the congregation and the congregation serves the community.)
- ➢ Whom does a medical office or doctor serve? Its patients.
- ➢ Whom does a professional service firm (e.g., accounting, engineering, law, or financial planning) serve? Its clients.
- ➢ Whom does a satellite TV company serve? Its subscribers.

What do these organizations have in common? They all have a *specific following*—a specific group made up of individuals who support the organization. They know exactly who they are and how to reach them. At any point in time they can view or print a list of all the individuals in their group of customers, complete with contact information.

Is Your Following a Vague List?

In the above examples, the group of followers is not vague, it is specific. Can you imagine a school not having a list of specific students, complete with name and detailed contact information? Would you let your kids go to a school that didn't keep track of its students?

Here's an example of a vague following. A local coffee shop owner was complaining about the lack of business. I asked him if he had a list of regular customers. He didn't. I then asked him to describe his regular customers. He said, "Anyone who comes to our area of town and likes coffee and enjoys socializing."

This coffee shop owner was loosely describing his target market. However, because he did not maintain a database of his regular patrons, he could not view or print a contact list. He could name a few customers, mostly by first name only.

In contrast, Starbucks builds their list by getting patrons to register their Rewards Card and using the Starbucks app. By obtaining contact information, Starbucks can now, at will, communicate by email with its patrons. (I love it when Starbucks sends me an email letting me know when I can get double stars on my rewards!)

Is your group of loyal followers a vague list or an actual list with specific names and contact information?

So what's the big deal with not having a specific list of your supporters? If you don't know exactly who your supporters are, you cannot communicate with them on a regular basis unless they are physically at your place of business. If you can't proactively communicate on a regular basis with each person in your following, then you will likely have tremendous difficulty building a loyal and lasting relationship with a sufficient number of people to support your business or your cause.

To connect with your followers and build lasting relationships you must be able to communicate with them at will. If you're not already doing so, start today building your list of followers—past customers, current customers, prospects, and your sphere of influence.

Questions for Growth

1. How would you describe your list of followers?
2. Do you have contact information, email or physical, for the people in your list of followers?
3. Do you keep in touch with your followers? How and when?
4. If you don't maintain a list of followers, how could you start one?
5. How could a list of loyal followers help grow your business?

18

TOP OF MIND

Have you ever purchased a vehicle, then everywhere you go you notice how many others own the exact same vehicle in the exact same color?

This happened to me when I bought a white Toyota 4-Runner. I saw it on the car lot and thought it was cool. I looked at others on the lot, but kept coming back to the white one. As soon as I drove it off the lot, I immediately noticed someone else had a white Toyota 4-Runner. On this one trip from the dealership to my home, I saw two other white Toyota 4-Runners. Over the next week I was thinking, "When did everyone go out and buy a white Toyota 4-Runner? How come I never noticed this before?"

Well, actually I had noticed this before, I just didn't realize it. Picture your mind as having two parts: your conscious mind and your subconscious mind. Your subconscious mind works in the background without much fanfare. It takes in and stores a gazillion times more information than your conscious mind. Your conscious mind is actually weak in comparison as it can only process the task at hand or think one thought at a time. In my example above, perhaps my subconscious mind had stored the fact that I had noticed white Toyota 4-Runners in the past and that I liked them. Also, now that I owned one and saw it every day, white Toyota 4-Runners became top-of-mind—this is when my conscious mind was notified. If my white Toyota 4-Runner is top-of-mind, why would I even notice or think about any other vehicle? I wouldn't. My conscious mind now notices white Toyota 4-Runners all day long.

How does this relate to you as a leader?

If you can create a positive, top-of-mind presence, you have a greater probability of creating positive influence. If you are a business owner or salesperson, what better way to build lasting relationships than to be top-of-mind. Here's an example.

Back in 2010 my wife and I were thinking about refinancing our mortgage. We had a rate in the mid- to high-4 percent range. At the time I heard rates were in the mid-3 percent range.

My wife said, "Who can we ask about it?"

"Hmm, I'm not sure," I replied, "I don't really know any mortgage people."

She says, "What about Juanita over at the bank? She sends us a newsletter every few months. I've actually kept a few because of the recipes she puts in the newsletters. Why don't you call her?"

"About a recipe?" I asked jokingly.

"No! About refinancing."

So I did. And Juanita ended up refinancing our mortgage.

If Juanita hadn't sent us newsletters, would she have been top-of-mind? Not hardly.

Often, when consumers are ready to buy, they don't always have a top-of-mind person in the related field. We didn't know a mortgage person. This happens more often than you might think, particularly with bigger-ticket items such as homes, mortgages, vehicles, financial services, and insurance. Unlike groceries, gas, or haircuts that are purchased frequently, these big-ticket items are not purchased frequently; therefore, people don't think about them as often. Why should they? But, when they're ready, wouldn't you want to be the one they think of?

Newsletters are just one way to stay in front of your following. While newsletters are not as personal as a handwritten note, they are highly effective for several reasons:

- Newsletters are an effective way to keep in touch with a large number of people.
- Newsletters are non-threatening. Readers lower their guard when reading newsletters because most newsletters are not a pitch-fest or a solicitation.
- Newsletters are not sales pitches.
- Newsletters contain interesting factoids.
- Newsletters contain items of interest such as recipes and community activities.
- Newsletters with humor, puzzles, and stories can be fun.
- Newsletters actively engage the reader.
- Newsletters tend to hang around longer than junk mail advertisements.
- Newsletters are shared.
- Newsletters can provide value related to the reader. Example: A real estate agent may include details about homes that have sold in the neighborhood. A homeowner can use this information by relating it to their own home. It also gets them thinking, "Hmmm, is now a good time to sell?"

- Newsletters are relatively inexpensive.
- Newsletters build familiarity when mailed consistently, whether monthly or quarterly.
- Newsletters can be physical mail or email. Physical mail tends to work better based on my personal experience. Besides, it's easier to obtain physical addresses than emails when targeting a specific geographic area.
- Newsletters generally have an implied sales pitch—"If you have questions, please feel free to call me. I'll certainly be glad to help if I can. Thank you!"
- Newsletters are "zero pressure."

Be realistic though, you're probably not going to get calls the first time you mail your newsletter. It will take some time, it could take a year or longer. Familiarity is built over time. The more someone becomes positively familiar with you, the more likely they'll think of you. And when will they think of you? They'll think of you when *their* timing is right. The key to making newsletters work is consistency. Consistency will help you become the top-of-mind person.

Newsletters are a great way for you to be in front of prospects in your target market, as well as your smaller, more personal group of contacts. For your smaller, more personal group, you can do even more to become top-of-mind. Let's say your smaller group consists of 100 to 200 people who have either done business with you in the past or are influencers who send you referrals. Besides newsletters, look for opportunities to make more personal connections, such as handwritten notes, relevant articles, personal phone calls, and personal visits. Again, these are not sales pitches, they are simply personal connections.

Nurturing your relationships with frequent and consistent communication builds positive familiarity. Positive familiarity builds trust. Is this the kind of connection you're looking for?

Questions for Growth

1. Has there ever been a time when you needed help with a big-ticket purchase, and you didn't really have a specific person in mind who was in that particular business?
2. If so, what process did you use to find someone who could help?
3. Would you like to be the top-of-mind person for people who seek your product or service?
4. What do you currently do, if anything, to become top-of-mind?
5. What could you do better to become top-of-mind?

19

RESPONSIBILITY TO MAINTAIN CONTACT

Whose responsibility is it to maintain contact?

If you want your grass to grow, you've got to water and fertilize it. No one else is going to water it for you. Don't expect people to keep up with your contact information, much less remember your name. It's your responsibility to maintain the relationship. Plain and simple.

In the past few chapters we've talked about your following and becoming top-of-mind. The best way to stay in front of them is simply to keep in touch.

Keeping in touch helps your following to gain and maintain familiarity with you and what you do. People are busy with life, they're under stress, and they certainly aren't sitting around thinking about you and me. Keeping in touch helps them remember that we're still here and ready to help, when they're ready.

How often should you keep in touch? If you're the leader, you want to stand out. The best way to stand out is to be there frequently and consistently. Once a year may not be enough. Daily might be too much. Depending on the nature of your work, perhaps monthly or quarterly would be better.

Responsibility to Maintain Contact

Remember the story about Bob, the tree guy, from chapter 17? Bob expected his past customers to remember him. Is this reasonable? Well, your customers have their own lives to live, and to be frank, remembering you is not at the top of their list. Besides, they may not need your service again for many years. With this in mind, is it even reasonable to expect your customers to remember you? No, you simply cannot leave it up to your customers to remember you.

If they won't remember you, how can it be their responsibility to maintain contact with you? It's not. To cut to the chase, it's not your customers' responsibility to maintain contact with you, it is your responsibility to maintain contact with them. Unlike a game of checkers where you take turns making a move, in business and sales it's *always* your move.

At a bare minimum, Bob the tree guy could have sent a simple postcard once a year, perhaps on Arbor Day (the last Friday in April). The postcard could include a helpful tip about caring for trees and shrubs. At least his past customers would hear from him once a year and would be more likely to remember him.

Communication

Building a relationship requires communication. Regular communication builds familiarity. The more your customers are familiar with you, the more you'll be top-of-mind the next time they need your help. Communicating with your customers is a must if you want them to remember you.

Also, what if you need to notify your customers of something important, like you've changed your address or phone number? This can happen more often than you might think. For example, one of my previous barbers changed salons without telling me. I found out when I called to make an appointment—the only information they would tell me was "She no longer works here." (At first I thought she was trying to ditch me as a customer!) When I found her, she told me she had a disagreement with the shop owner and decided to leave immediately. She said, "I'm very sorry I wasn't able to let you know where I moved, but I didn't have your contact information." (Just so you'll know, she never asked for it.)

This happens often. People change employers all the time. I know financial advisors, real estate agents, automobile salespersons, and insurance agents who have worked for every employer in town.

How will your clients be able to find you unless you're able to provide them with your new contact information? For this most basic reason, you must be able to communicate important information with your customers, clients, supporters, or followers. And to communicate, you must maintain a contact list.

Trust

A loyal following is a group of people who trust you. They trust you to help them, to take care of them, and to treat them like you'd treat your own mother. As mentioned above, and to repeat for emphasis, building a relationship requires communication. Regular communication builds familiarity. And *positive* familiarity builds trust.

And that's how connections are built—through trust.

If you build trust with each of your loyal followers, they will see you as their trusted advisor, regardless of your field. When they trust you, they'll come back to you for help again and again, and they'll refer others to you as well.

Your Greatest Asset

What is the greatest asset as a leader?

Many business people immediately jump to their balance sheet and start naming assets such as cash, inventory, accounts receivable, equipment, or real estate. However, these assets were derived or acquired because of your greatest asset—your loyal followers. Specifically, if you're in sales, your sales and profits originate from your followers. Without your followers what do you have?

Business people often do whatever it takes to protect or insure their inventory, equipment, real estate, and even key employees. But what are they doing to protect their customer-base from eroding? Often very little, other than to provide good service, and perhaps only when it is requested. Providing service when requested by a customer is being reactive—they request, you react. What we're talking about is being proactive—you reach out to them through consistent communication.

If you don't protect your customer-base, one-by-one your customers will buy from someone else. Why allow this when it's so easy to prevent? The way to avoid this is for you to be the top-of-mind person in your customer's mind. Communicate, communicate, communicate. Spend a little money and send a monthly newsletter, a birthday card, or a holiday card. Do something, anything, to show them you care enough about their relationship to keep in touch. If you don't show how much you care, they'll find someone who does.

A friend of mine, Alan, is an accountant. He keeps up with accounting firms that are for sale. I asked him how these firms are valued since they don't have inventory or much equipment. He said the firms are valued based on a multiple of gross revenue. I then asked, "Since you don't get an inventory or equipment list, what exactly are you buying?"

Alan replied, "You'd better get a detailed client list. That's the only proof the firm actually exists." He's right about that.

Accountants realize the value of the firm is based on their greatest asset—their clients. If you were an accountant, would you buy a firm if you didn't know exactly who was on the client list *and* be able to communicate with them? No way Jose'!

Your customers, clients, supporters, and followers *are* your greatest asset. The best way to protect your greatest asset is to communicate regularly to show them you care.

Now, to take this further, in my opinion, if you have employees, then your employees are actually your greatest asset. Your employees represent your company and are the frontline, or face, of your organization. When you invest in your employees to become a customer-oriented army, you will have your whole team working in unison to build a loyal following of customers.

Summary

If you don't know exactly who your followers are, you can't communicate with them on a regular basis. How can you build a relationship with someone if you can't communicate with them?

It's always your move. You simply cannot leave it up to your customers to remember you, nor expect them to be loyal to you—that's your job!

In real estate, the mantra is "location, location, location." If you want to be the leader in your field, your mantra should be "communication, communication, communication." Communication equals connection.

Questions for Growth

1. How do you feel about your responsibility to maintain contact?
2. In the past, how would you describe your efforts to maintain contact? (Use Bob, the tree guy as a comparison.)
3. How do you feel about your followers being your greatest asset?
4. How do you feel about your employees being your greatest asset?
5. What are you doing to protect your followers from going elsewhere?
6. How can you improve your efforts to maintain contact with your followers?

20

PLANNING BY OBJECTIVE

You know the saying, *you're too close to the forest to see the trees?* Sometimes, if not many times, we get too close to the thing we're doing to see the big picture. There are several reasons why this happens.

- ➤ Life is busy. When you're busy as a bee it's easier to focus on getting stuff done than to see the big picture.
- ➤ Things get complicated in a hurry. In business we tend to make things more complicated than necessary. The more complicated the process, the more difficult to see the big picture.
- ➤ Stress causes us to lose sight of what's most important. When you're stressed, putting out the fires that cause the stress tend to become the focus. We put bandages on the situation rather than fix the root problem.
- ➤ Inside-the-box thinking causes us to lose site of the big picture. In general, people have a natural inclination to look for the obvious, inside-the-box answer. Have you ever told someone you were sick and their first response was, "Have you taken anything?" You want to say, "Wow, what a novel idea. Why didn't I think of that?"

Leaders must keep sight of the big picture. Life will get busy, things will get complicated, stress will raise its ugly head, and people will naturally look inside the box. As a leader what can you do?

First, determine the objective. What needs to be accomplished? What is the big picture?

Second, keep the objective in front of you at all times. For any and all tasks, ask yourself if this will help achieve the objective. For administrative tasks set aside a certain amount of time to get them done, preferably not during your most effective work hours. When the pre-determined amount of time is up, stop working on the admin tasks and get on with your more important work.

Third, develop a plan based on the objective. I know that seems obvious, but if you've been in business any length of time, you understand how quickly things can deviate from the desired path.

Here's a nonbusiness example in my personal life to demonstrate how easy it is to lose sight of the objective. When I turned 40 I noticed a few things happening with my health. I had gained more than a few extra pounds. At first this didn't seem like such a big deal because everyone tends to gain weight as they age. The next thing that happened was my biometric numbers (blood pressure, cholesterol, pulse, BMI) were getting to the borderline high range. My doctor's immediate answer was to put me on medication. Sure, that's the obvious, inside-the-box answer. But I wanted to look at alternatives, like diet and exercise.

I wasn't much for exercise and I love to eat good food. Combine that with a desk job and you have a recipe for poor health. So I began researching diet and exercise ideas. As I did my research, *losing weight* kept coming to my mind as the main objective because it seemed to be the obvious answer. But was losing weight really the objective, or was the objective actually achieving *better health*? In my case it was achieving better health; losing weight was a side benefit. The more healthy foods I ate and the more I would exercise, the more weight I'd lose.

Now, many of us have a tendency to jump in and go crazy with diet and exercise. By "go crazy" I mean we go to ridiculous extremes, kind of like we do with New Year's resolutions. We can go for about a week, or maybe a month, but then we're right back where we started. Lack of time, insufficient will power, and disdain for exercise and eating healthy foods are the key culprits that make these extreme plans unsustainable. As humans we tend to overcomplicate things a bit.

I needed a simple, sustainable plan to become healthier. That's it. As for the eating habits, I focused on natural, plant-based foods rather than processed foods. My reasoning, which I derived from my quick research, was that nutrition comes from plants, not processed foods. I'm not perfect by any means, but I eat way more plant-based foods and much less processed foods than I used to. However, the example I want to share is about my exercise plan.

I'm busy, I have no time, and I hate to exercise. I tried going to a gym. It took too long to get ready, travel to the gym, do an exercise routine, and then leave the gym, shower, and change back into my normal street clothes. Although I got a great deal on an annual gym membership, I only went once. From a cost-benefit analysis, that was one expensive trip to the gym.

I tried working out with weights at home. Again, time was the main issue. Also, my weights were in my workshop which was not insulated—it was hot in the summer and cold in the winter. I dreaded it.

I tried watching workout programs on DVD. That just wasn't for me.

We didn't have a workout room so I had to exercise in the den. Besides my wife and kids watching me, talking to me, and making fun of me, I also kept falling over the coffee table. I needed a better plan.

Then it hit me. What was my objective? It was not to build my physique so I could look like an underwear model (my wife, however, said that should be my objective). Nor was my objective to become strong. Sure, weightlifting can improve your health and I have nothing against it, but my problem was one of efficiency. I needed something that would improve my blood pressure, pulse, and cholesterol in as little time per day as possible.

As mentioned in chapter 2, at age 49 I decided to start jogging. I decided on jogging because of something I learned in my teens from one of my lawn mowing customers, Mr. Rogers. It seemed like Mr. Rogers was going for a run every time I mowed his lawn. One day I asked if he ran marathons. He said, "No, I run just one mile every day, weather permitting."

This was not the answer I expected. "Why just one mile?" I asked.

He said, "Because it keeps me healthy." Further, he said, "I don't particularly like running, I just do it to stay healthy. I don't take medications and I've never been in the hospital."

His answer must've had some influence on me because I remembered it after all these years. So, at age 49 I decided to take up jogging.

The last time I had run was probably in high school. To get prepared I bought some decent running shoes and downloaded a running app. The first time I got out there I stretched for a few minutes and took off out of my driveway. After about 15 seconds I felt like I was about to puke. My heart was pounding out of my chest and my calves felt like they were about to explode. My calves were so tight I couldn't bend my foot at the ankle. They were stiff as a board. I looked like a goof ball walking home on my heels. For some reason I opened the running app—I had jogged for a grand total of .01 miles. Not one-tenth of a mile, but one-hundredth of a mile! Talk about discouraged!

That first outing made me realize why I hate running. I wanted to give up. But instead of giving up, I took out a sheet of paper and came up with a plan.

> Week one—jog for 15 seconds per day. Since jogging a mile seemed impossible I decided to jog for 15 seconds a day for the first week. Understandably, my wife laughed at me. But, after a week I could jog for 15 seconds without feeling like I would throw up. My lungs and calves had acclimated to the short jog. I was ready to step it up.

> Week two—jog for 30 seconds per day. Now, going from 15 seconds to 30 seconds doesn't sound like much, but my mind and body were screaming, "That's twice as far! How can you do that!"

It wasn't easy, but I did the 30 seconds every day for a week. And, I didn't die.

- ➤ Week three—jog for 45 seconds per day. It wasn't as hard as the leap from 15 to 30 seconds, but it was still hard.
- ➤ Week four—jog for 60 seconds per day. Still not easy, but it wasn't near as difficult as the previous increases.
- ➤ Week five—jog for 90 seconds per day. Then, a miracle happened near the end of week five—I just kept going. Somehow I was able to jog for half a mile. According to the running app I jogged the half mile in about eight minutes. A half mile in eight minutes is laughable I know; I just couldn't believe I had jogged for a continuous eight minutes! I was excited.
- ➤ Week six—jog for one mile. By the end of week six I had finally jogged one mile. This was the first continuous mile I had run since junior high!

I was so excited about my accomplishment that I made the mistake of posting it on Facebook. Yes, I received a lot of "Likes" and congratulations. The problem was all the questions about when I was going to run a 5k, 10k, half-marathon, or a whole marathon. I even received links about upcoming 5k fundraisers. Without much thinking I went into—training mode. I started trying to see how fast I could run the mile. Then I'd try to run further than a mile. After a few weeks, I had stopped altogether. I had lost sight of my original objective. (By the way, this is the point of this story—losing sight of the objective.)

My wife, my hero, encouraged me. She said, "You have come such a long way. Forget about becoming a runner and get out there and jog your mile."

So I did exactly that. My objective was to get healthy, not to run marathons. I tweaked my plan a bit and started jogging 15 minutes a day for three to five days a week. That's it. After about a year of this I got a huge surprise when I applied for some life insurance. I figured I'd get a standard rating, but I didn't. Based on the numbers from my latest physical, I got the highest rating possible, preferred plus! I would've thought that I'd have to be a marathoner to get a preferred plus rating, but I did it by jogging just 15 minutes a day and eating more plant-based foods and less processed foods. That's it. No long hours in the gym, no spinning classes, and no cross-fit.

Yes, I could've continued to increase my jogging distance, but based on my experience, I believe the benefits would've increased at a diminishing rate. Besides, I didn't have a lot of time—the 15 minutes met my need for efficiency. *Distance* was not important; *rate* was not important; only *time* was important. I wasn't competing with anyone else, or even myself—I was just jogging 15 minutes per day. Applying the time consistently, 3 to 5 days per week, gave me *my* desired results. To say this another way—you don't have to be a marathon runner to get major benefits from jogging. (Thank you Mr. Rogers!)

What's funny is, when the topic of jogging comes up, the first thing people ask me is the obvious, "When are you going to run a marathon?"

My answer, "I'm not. I'm jogging to improve my health." And when I try to explain it, people just look at me like I've lost my mind. But I haven't; I'm getting the exact results to achieve my objective. Why complicate it?

The point is not to give you advice about diet and exercise; I'm not qualified to do that. The point is to always keep your objective front and center. Let the objective determine the plan. Start with the objective before you start doing the work. Then, let the objective guide your way.

You know, you really can do just about anything you set your mind to, if you come up with a plan and stick to it, no matter how ridiculous it seems. I don't consider myself a runner. Running is not what I call fun. I don't see how people run for miles and miles and make it look easy. However, as much as I hate running, I do see the value for my health. I could've easily given up after that first day of jogging. My mind and body were screaming, "Quit, you fool! Running sucks!" Instead, I came up with a workable plan. Most people thought that jogging for 15 seconds was ridiculous (some even laughed). But, starting with 15 seconds is exactly what I needed to do to get to where I wanted to be. Interestingly, those that laughed didn't exercise at all.

If you're the leader, people will look to you to keep things on track and moving in the right direction. The way to improve your connections is to communicate the objective clearly and to ask for input and ideas. When people feel that they're involved, they'll take greater pride in pursuing the objective.

Questions for Growth

1. Do you ever feel so busy that you lose sight of the big picture?
2. What is it that's creating the busy work in your life?
3. At work, what is your main objective?
4. Is that really your main objective? (What are some other possible objectives?)
5. Do you have other work responsibilities that aren't necessarily related to your main objective? (Paperwork, reports, admin, accounting, training, etc.)
6. How could you structure your day to prevent the "other responsibilities" from controlling your day?
7. How can you apply this to your personal life? What is your main objective (with your relationships, your health, your finances)?

8. How can you stay focused on your main objective to be most effective at what matters most?

21

RESULTS-ORIENTED VS PEOPLE-ORIENTED

Leaders have many responsibilities. Ultimately, these responsibilities boil down to two categories: managing results and managing people.

Which is more important, managing results or managing people?

Managing results is basically managing tasks, or getting things done. Leaders who focus on managing results tend to be goal-oriented or task-oriented. Getting the job done is the number one priority, even before the needs of the people. These leaders tend to come up with a plan of action then disseminate the plan to the troops. The troops are then held accountable to produce results according to the plan.

On the other hand, managing people is about managing relationships. Leaders who focus on managing relationships tend to show concern for people and the morale of the group. This leader is sensitive to, or at least aware of, emotions. Often the awareness comes from being communicative, not just toward the group as a whole, but toward individuals within the group. The relationship-oriented leader may also be considered nurturing, helpful, considerate, nice, and great to work with.

What type of leader are you, results-oriented or people-oriented?

Not sure? Well, to be honest, this is sort of a trick question. Let me explain. Leaders tend to have a dominant style—results or people. However, the style is not always one way or the other—it's somewhere in between. Let's change the question slightly. What type of leadership do you lean toward (your more dominant style), results-oriented or people-oriented?

Another question, which style is more important, results or people? Achieving the desired result is important. You may lose your job if you and your team don't achieve the objective. After all, as the leader, you're responsible, right? However, people are also important. People tend to work better (harder, smarter, more efficiently, more effectively, and so on) when they feel they're important to the leader, the group, and the task. People can make or break your results.

To be an effective leader, it's important to be aware of your dominant style. There are situations when your dominant style can actually work against you. What if you are more of a results-oriented leader, but the situation calls for more attention to the needs of the people? Are you the right leader for the situation or would another leader be more effective?

Before you answer definitively, perhaps you might be willing to adapt your style. Yes, change your dominant style.

Sometimes people are promoted to a leadership position because of their ability to get things done. The promotion can be a sense of confirmation that getting things done is the way to be a good leader. However, being promoted from one position to a higher position may actually change the situation. A different situation may call for a different leadership style. In addition to the situation, the people may also need a different type of leader.

For this reason it's important for leaders to adapt to their situation and to the needs of the people. Let's say you lead a technical group of well-trained and highly-experienced individuals and you're assigned to complete a project in 18 months. Because of your team members' skills and experience level, they may not need as much personal attention as a low-skill level and inexperienced team. However, because the project has an 18 month time frame, you definitely don't want to ignore the needs of your team. Each person on your team still needs to feel they're important and that you care. Also, because your team may be closer to the project than you are, they may be able to provide you with valuable information to help keep the project moving forward. What if they run into an obstacle or sticking point? What if their resources are running low? What if your team members are getting burned out? This is where communication with, and attention to, your team are necessary to keep everyone on the same page and the project on track.

Let's turn this scenario around. What if you're leading team members who have little training or experience. This is common with entry-level jobs and with volunteer organizations. Although you may have certain performance results to attain, your team will likely need lots of your attention. They may need assurance, encouragement, appreciation, as well as how-to training. In an entry-level, low-paying job, it's not uncommon for management to feel that each position/person can easily be replaced. Therefore, little attention is given to each person—either they perform or they're replaced. High turnover rates may be an indicator that this is happening. In general, people take pride in what they do, particularly when they feel that what they're doing is important. They need guidance to feel they're doing their job properly. They need encouragement to stay motivated. And they need to know you care. Again, communication is the key.

Whether your dominant style is results-oriented or people-oriented, it's not only important to be aware of your style, but to be able to adapt your style to the situation and to the needs of the people. First, assess the people and the situation to determine what type of leadership might work best. Some people need more direction, others need less. Some jobs are more ambiguous, others are straightforward. Some jobs are repetitive, others are individualized. Some jobs are simple, others are complicated. Some people have more experience, others have less. Some jobs are volunteer, others are paid. Once you've assessed the situation and the needs of the group as a whole, make a determination of the leadership style that would work best.

By communicating (listening more than you talk) with each person, or with the managers if you have a large group, you'll get a sense of how the people are feeling and what they need from you. Also, look at the situation to determine which style might work better. For instance, how you lead a group of soldiers would be totally different than how you lead your family at home. Of course, that's an example of extremely different situations. In real life, however, the different situations may not be as clear.

Find your balance. An adaptive leader balances results and people. Remember, it takes people to get results. Treat each individual as a person. Show them you care, show them appreciation, and make them feel important. One of the best ways to connect with people is to communicate, particularly the listening part.

Questions for Growth

1. Which group of people would be more likely to perform better?

Group A - The people on this team feel you are driven. They don't feel like you are concerned about their needs. You seldom interact, much less carry on a conversation, with the individuals on the team. They do not feel appreciated. They gossip and complain to one another. They know they have a job to do, but their desire and energy level are low. Morale of the group is low.

Group B - The people on this team know you care. They feel appreciated. They feel comfortable talking to you and/or management. They feel heard. They say you are kind and considerate. Not only do they feel encouraged, they encourage one another. Energy levels are high. Morale of the group is high.

2. Which is your dominant style, results-oriented or people-oriented?
3. Are there situations where your dominant style may not be what's called for?
4. If you're aware of your dominant-style, what can you do to work

on, or emphasize, your subordinate style?
5. How can you use communication to assess the situation and the needs of your team?

References and Sources:

Northouse, Peter G., *Leadership: Theory and Practice* (Sage Publications, Inc., 5th Edition, 2010), chapter 5-Situational Approach

22

DON'T GET INVOLVED

To make connections it's important to get involved in community activities such as a civic or service club, chamber of commerce, and church. Or is it important?

One of the old marketing methods of many business professionals was (and still is) to do just that, get involved in many community activities. The more activities you're involved in, the more people ask you to get involved in something else. You could make a career out of serving your community.

I know an accountant who was involved in a civic club, the chamber, his church, and he was on every non-profit board in town. I just didn't understand how he had the time to do all that. When his name would come up in conversation, I'd ask how this person could serve in so many capacities. The typical reply was, "Well, when he shows up to a meeting he's great."

Hearing that gave me relief because I felt guilty that I couldn't serve any more than I was already serving—I was just too dadgum busy. Now, to be honest, the guilt was not really about being able to serve more. Sure the cause is important, but, quite frankly, many business people, including myself, get involved with community activities in order to meet people.

And it's not just community activities, people today are busier than ever before. I don't mean they're working harder, they're just busier. People seem to be involved in way too many things. And the result is stress and dissatisfaction. Why? Well, I'm not a professional of the mind, I'm just speaking from my personal experience and what I've observed with some of my peers. Here's my point of view—people are *involved* in many things, but they're truly *engaged* in very little.

So what's the difference in getting involved and getting engaged because they sound similar? Let me share a couple examples.

My first example that opened my eyes was in 1998 when I went through a divorce. At the time I wasn't really sure what went wrong. So, *after* my divorce I read quite a few relationship books. In hindsight, it would have been more helpful if I'd read them *before* the divorce.

The reason I wasn't sure what went wrong was because we didn't fight and we didn't argue. At the time I thought that was a good thing. But after reading all those relationship books, a light bulb came on—I realized that although I was *involved* in my marriage, I really wasn't *engaged* in my marriage.

Another example happened after I had remarried. We had two kids, a boy and a girl, 14 months apart. When they were about 3 and 4 years old we took them on a family beach trip to St. George Island, Florida.

Now, my idea of going to the beach is to sit in my beach chair and relax. I like to sit under my umbrella, listen to my 80s playlist, and just chill. But, if you've ever taken your kids to the beach, you know how it is. Every five minutes, "Daddy, Daddy can you get in the water with me?" "Daddy, will you build a sandcastle with me?"

Well, about halfway through the day, I yelled over to the kids from my beach chair, "Hey kids, are ya'll having a good time at the beach?"

My son runs over to my chair and says something that felt like a punch in the stomach. He says, "Yes sir, but it'd be a lot more fun if you'd get in the sand and play with us."

He was right! I thought I was *involved* with my kids by taking them to the beach, but to my son's point, I wasn't *engaged* with my kids at all.

I used marriage and kids to demonstrate the difference between involved and engaged. But, it also applies to other areas in your life:

- ➤ Work—When you're hired, you're involved, but that doesn't mean you're engaged in your work. At first people tend to be excited and enthusiastic about a new job. They're excited to learn new things and change the world. Changing the world may be a slight exaggeration; perhaps we should say they're excited about the opportunity and the future potential. But after a while the new wears off, it's easy to just go through the motions day-in and day-out.
- ➤ Church—When you join and attend church, you're involved. However, joining and attending just puts your name on the roles, it doesn't mean you're engaged.
- ➤ Community, chamber, and civic clubs—When you join, pay dues, and attend meetings you're doing the bare minimum to be involved. Just because you married the club, doesn't mean you're engaged in the club.

These examples may strike a nerve with you, but I promise I'm not trying to step on your toes. I'm simply trying to articulate the difference between being involved and being engaged. They seem similar, but there's a big difference between the two.

The problem with being involved, but not engaged, seems to be a lack of meaning or fulfillment. When you're involved in many things, it's almost impossible to get excited or find the meaning in any one thing. How can you get excited or find the meaning in something when all you're doing is showing up? Have you ever stopped to think about how many things you're involved in, particularly things where all you're doing is showing up (if you show up at all)?

The bottom line is that many people just seem to be involved in way too many things, but they're truly engaged in very little. I get it, I'm busy, you're busy, we're all busy. People are always asking you to volunteer for something and we hate to say "No," but at the same time, we simply don't have time to engage in everything.

So what can you do? Maybe this will help.

Not long after I started dating my wife, Heather, people started pressuring me, I mean *asking* us "When are ya'll getting married?"

Once we got married, people would ask, "When are ya'll having kids?" Of course like most newlyweds we'd say, "Well, we just want to enjoy our time together first."

After a year or so, the question became more intense, especially from our parents, "When in the heck are ya'll having kids?" And we'd say, "Well, we're trying to save up some money first."

And every single time we'd say that, we got some advice—"Kids are expensive. If you're waiting to have a baby until you can afford it, you never will."

I share this with you because it applies to many things that we know we need to do, but we're waiting for that special moment. For most people it's waiting until you're no longer busy. If you're waiting until you're no longer busy, you never will be.

If you want to be more effective as a leader, more effective in your work, and more effective in your family, it's time to stop being involved and start getting engaged. Here are some ideas to help.

> Drop some things. Yep, you already know this; now just do it. Make a list of all the activities you're involved in. What's most important and what's least important? Either drop the least important activities now, or do it slowly. If you want to do it slowly, drop one now, adjust, then drop another next month or next quarter. Also, if you're serving in a position for a certain term, you could wait until the term expires to drop the activity. The fewer activities you're involved in, the easier it will be to engage in one or two.

> Only engage in activities and groups you feel strongly about. The more strongly you feel, the more meaning and fulfillment you'll experience.

> ➤ Manage your energy. We often try to manage our time. Typically we're trying to see how much more we can fit in our schedule by managing our time better. I know I've been guilty of this. Rather than managing your time, try managing your energy. Do this by taking short breaks throughout the day, don't cram your schedule, create transition times between activities, exercise or walk to release tension, and get plenty of rest each night (or each day if you're on the night shift). An increased energy level will help you become more engaged throughout the day.

> ➤ Focus. Most really successful people got there because they focused. Think Bill Gates, Warren Buffett, Michael Jordan, Tiger Woods, and Tom Brady, to name a few. What are these individuals known for? One thing or three things? Just one. When you focus on something, put everything you've got into mastery. Learn all you can, practice relentlessly, and seek professional coaching. Focusing is how you engage in your work.

> ➤ Help employees further their career by providing a path of growth. Often employers overlook the fact that many employees, even in entry-level positions, would like to move up. If there's no path to move up, these people often feel stuck. This leads to dissatisfaction and boredom. Think of yourself as a coach—ask them about their current job as well as their aspirations. Once you know where they want to go, you can provide a path of growth. Even if all you can provide is encouragement, it gives them hope and makes them feel you care. This is how you can engage with your employees, the people you manage, or the people on your team.

In summary, being involved in too many activities is like going a mile wide, but only one inch deep. Engaging is like going one inch wide and a mile deep. You'll never strike oil by skimming the surface. Think of depth as fulfillment, meaning, happiness, growth, and mastery. The deeper you dig, the more you'll discover.

It's difficult to become really connected with any one thing or any one person when you're spread too thin. Engaging in fewer activities and engaging with people will help strengthen your connections with your work, your co-workers, your customers, your community, and your family.

Questions for Growth

1. Do you feel that you are spread too thin?
2. Are you involved in a lot of activities?
3. Do you feel you're engaged, or just involved?
4. What activities are most important to you?
5. Who is most important to you?

6. Are there activities you need to drop?
7. How can you be more engaged in your work?
8. How can you be more engaged in your community activities?
9. How can you be more engaged with your family?

23

THE PEOPLE BUSINESS

My dad was in life insurance sales for most of his career. Over the years, he taught me some valuable lessons and shared some really cool stories. On many occasions he'd let me tag along on a sales call, seminar, or a vacation he had qualified for because of his production.

Dad was a top producer, which often led to speaking engagements. Agents always wanted to know his "secret." One of the most memorable things I heard him say was to a group of insurance agents.

Dad began his speech with, "First and foremost, to be successful in sales, you must know what business you're in."

I was a typical teenager who thought I was smarter than my parents. I was also embarrassed by everything they did. So as I listened to him say this opening line I thought, *"How ridiculous! These folks obviously know they're in the insurance business."*

Then Dad asked the audience, "What business are you actually in?"

No one said a word, but neither did Dad. After what seemed like an eternity, one of the sales managers raised his hand and said, "I guess we're in the insurance business."

"Yes, you do sell insurance," Dad replied, "anyone else?"

Another agent raised her hand and said, "We're in the life insurance business."

Then, Dad said, "Yes, you sell insurance, specifically life insurance. But let's take a much higher view." Dad continued, "Regardless of the product or service you sell, every business has one thing in common—people. And you know this is true because it is people who buy all products or services. What business are you in? You are in the *people* business. Your job as a life insurance sales person is to help people. You help people find solutions to their problems and desires."

I am grateful to have heard this message at such an early age. I believe it altered my perspective about the sales field from a view of product-peddling to one of people-helping. One is pushy and the other is professional.

I heard this message again in a quote from Howard Schultz, Founder and CEO of Starbucks. Schultz says, "We are not in the coffee business serving people, we are in the people business serving coffee."

What a great way to put it! Try it with your business. The life insurance agents my Dad worked with could say "We are not in the life insurance business serving people, we are in the people business serving life insurance."

Regardless of what type of business you're in, there are three questions you must be able to answer.

1. What product or service do you sell?
2. Who buys, or needs, your product?
3. What problem or desire does your product solve?

If you can answer these three questions with clarity, then you're well on your way to helping more people solve their problems and pursue their desires. And when you do that, you'll be rewarded. The key to it all is helping people. And you can't help people sufficiently until you understand people effectively.

People skills are a prerequisite to serving people. And the cool thing is, people skills can be learned. Do you know a people person? What makes them a people person? Do you consider yourself a people person? Being a people person doesn't mean you have to be an extrovert, outgoing, or a social butterfly. Being a people person means being approachable, sincere, and concerned. Show you care, be genuine, and most of all, listen to what people have to say.

Start today by making a commitment to improve your people skills. To learn people skills, probably the best people book of all time is *How to Win Friends and Influence People* by Dale Carnegie. Better yet, get the audio version and listen to it once a year. Think of it as your personal, people skills coach.

Remember, whatever business you're in, you're in the people business first. A business or organization cannot connect with people. People connect with people.

Questions for Growth

1. What business are you in?
2. What product or service do you (or your company) sell?
3. How do you serve people?
4. How can you serve people first?
5. What people skills would help you be more effective?

References and Sources:

o   Bolton Ph.D, Robert, *People Skills: How to Assert Yourself, Listen to Others, and Resolve Conflicts* (Simon & Schuster, Inc, 1986)
o   Carnegie, Dale, *How to Win Friends and Influence People* (Pocket Books, a division of Simon and Schuster, Inc., 1982)

24

RESPONSIBILITY

Leadership is a role of responsibility. Leaders are responsible for results, performance, growth, vision, direction, timeliness, problems, obstacles, solutions, resources, culture, people, and morale. Basically, leaders are pretty much responsible for everything.

Leaders may delegate activities, but ultimate responsibility remains with the leader. If the leader can choose the person for the task, then the leader is responsible for choosing the *right* person for the task. If the leader is responsible for training and supervising, then the leader is responsible for providing *adequate* training and supervision. The leader is responsible for providing *sufficient* resources to get the job done. The leader is also responsible for *helping* the team overcome obstacles. No matter how you slice it, it's almost impossible for a leader to shirk responsibility.

That brings us to an important point—when things go awry, good leaders don't cast blame. Blaming is a defense mechanism. It is much easier to blame someone or something else than to take responsibility. The problem with blaming others is that it destroys trust with those you're leading. Trust is built over time, one connection at a time. Trust must be earned. Yet, trust can be broken in the blink of an eye. Once trust is broken it's almost impossible to restore.

Good leaders accept the responsibility when something doesn't go as planned. They admit it, they accept it, and they own it. Yes, there may have been reasons supporting why something didn't go as planned, and it's okay to share those reasons. But, rather than cast blame on a particular person or persons, phrase the blame as "I" or "we." As the leader you're front and center; you're the representative and spokesperson. When it comes to blame, name no names.

What if you need to address the issue with someone or several people on your team? If so, address it in private. Your automatic response might be to chastise the people who made the blunder. If it was reckless or willful, perhaps chastising is necessary. A better course would be to get an assessment of what happened, why it happened, and ask "How can we prevent this from happening again?" Instruction works better than criticism. Business is an ongoing experiment to learn what works and what doesn't. Sometimes things just don't work. The important thing to ask is "What did we learn from this?"

To build strength in your team, each person on your team needs to know you've got their back. Think of yourself as the buffer. You're the punching bag for the team. That's pretty much why you're the leader; you must be ready, willing, and able to take on the leadership role. When the individuals on your team feel your support, something transformational happens—they become willing to work more diligently and take on greater responsibility for you and the team. You build a mutual respect that strengthens your individual connections, which strengthens the entire team.

When we blame others there's an underlying belief that this somehow makes us look smarter. By casting blame on the other person, it supposedly shows that they're incapable and should be held responsible for the error. Then, in turn, this supposedly makes you look like the hero, as if you discovered the problem and who to blame. Not so. Not so at all. It actually makes you look weak in your leadership and trustworthiness.

In business, responsibility is not about finding fault. It's about acknowledging what happened and how it can be corrected. Most mistakes and failures made in the course of business are not criminal in nature, therefore, no one needs to be sent before the firing squad. When you acknowledge something, you're admitting the failure, describing what has been learned from the experience, and stating how this will help in the future.

Here's the deal—leaders don't have to be perfect. Leaders make mistakes, too. What's the difference? The difference is that good leaders don't blame and they don't make excuses—they own it. Whatever went wrong was not intentional and we're working on a way to rectify the situation. We learned from the experience and will use this information going forward. If the situation calls for an apology, then apologize without making excuses.

Leadership is not about you and your goals. Leadership is about the group and the common goals of the group. You're the captain. Whatever happens on the ship is your responsibility. Storms will surely come and you must be prepared to weather the storms like a tenured captain.

Problems with leaders can occur when the leader is leading for personal gain. In this case, the leader's primary objective is to get ahead. A self-centered leader may be more inclined to blame others than a leader who is focused on the group. Although promotion and monetary gain may be benefits to leadership, they're side benefits. These things must be earned by demonstrating your leadership abilities. This means acting like a leader first; the rewards will come later.

Being a leader doesn't mean you have all the answers. But, not knowing the answer doesn't mean you're not responsible. You're expected to get the answer. You may need to do some research, learn something new, or better yet, look to your team. This is where you must rely on others. Let's say you're the leader for a technical project. However, you don't have the technical skills to do the job yourself. Maybe *your* training is in management or administration area. Hopefully, there are people on your team who have the technical training and skills to perform the work. Look to your team for ideas. Brainstorm together. You may have to make the final decision on which direction to go, even when you rely on others for the answers, but no matter what, it's still your responsibility.

A responsible leader never assumes they know all there is to know. First of all, it's impossible to know everything or to have experienced everything. Yet, someone on your team may have more knowledge or experience in a certain area than you. A good leader is open to new and different ideas. You've heard the saying *think outside the box*. Well, forget the box. Assume there is no box at all. So what if that's the way it's always been done! So what if this way or that way is what's most acceptable! As long as mankind has been around and as long as mankind will exist, there will always be new possibilities.

A responsible leader not only owes responsibility to his or her group, but also to the organization, supporters, customers, vendors, creditors, board of directors, shareholders, and the public. How do you fulfill responsibility to so many different groups? Be honest, tell the truth, and accept responsibility. This means building trust with each of these relationships. Everyone to whom you owe a responsibility must know they can rely on you, not necessarily for an ideal outcome (success), but for you to do what you say you'll do, when you say you'll do it.

To strengthen your connections with your team and all the other groups to whom you're responsible, let integrity define you—be honest, tell the truth, and above all, own it.

Questions for Growth

1. How would you describe your responsibilities as a leader?
2. Do you agree that the ultimate responsibility falls on the leader?
3. Has someone ever blamed you for something, whether or not you were at fault? How did it make you feel? Did it affect your trust for the person who blamed you?
4. Have you ever felt the need to blame someone else? Can you describe a specific situation?

5. How do you feel about accepting full responsibility, even when you must rely on others to get the job done?
6. How can you communicate to those you lead that you have their back?
7. How can you demonstrate that you have their back?

25

SHARE THE CREDIT

In the previous chapter we talked about leaders taking responsibility when things go wrong. But what about when things go right?

More often than not, we're more likely to point out the negative than to point out the positive. Why? Because the negative is disruptive to our pattern of expectations. We expect things to go as planned. But when things go off course, we act as if we're surprised.

- ➤ Have you ever planned for a trip to take three hours, but due to traffic and bathroom breaks it took four hours?
- ➤ Have you ever estimated the time for a project to take 30 minutes, but it takes two hours instead?
- ➤ Have you ever estimated the cost for a project to be a certain amount, but it ends up costing twice as much than you expected?
- ➤ Have you ever left on time to get to your next appointment, but end up breaking your neck to get there?

That's life! Life is not perfect and very little will go exactly as planned. Yet, we are so freaked out when things go wrong.

On the other hand, when things go right we hardly notice. We show no emotion. We simply move on to the next thing. Why don't we celebrate when things go smoothly? I'll give you an example. I remember asking my wife "How come you never point out the good things that I do?" She replied, "Because that's what you're supposed to do." That's when it hit me. We don't pay much attention when things go right because that's how we think it should be. We may not necessarily think things will go as planned, but when they do we believe that's how it should be.

To summarize our human idiosyncrasies, when things go right, we think that's how it should be; when things go wrong, we're somehow surprised.

Now, let's get real. If you continuously focus on the negative, then the negative will grow. If you focus on the positive, then the positive will grow.

It's like the story about the fight between two wolves. One wolf is evil and the other is good. Which wolf will win the fight? Simple, the one you feed. If you want to experience more joy and happiness out of life, get real. Setbacks are a part of life, don't get so upset when they happen. Instead, focus on what went right.

You may need to create buffers to allow for the unexpected. Allow more time than necessary, add a little extra cushion to your cost estimate, and cut people some slack—they will have setbacks, too. If someone says they'll be there in ten minutes, give them twenty. Things happen; plan for the unplanned.

Okay, let's shift gears. If you're leading a group, you may exhibit the same negative/positive mentality as we just described. For example, you may notice when people mess up more than you notice when they do things right. Why? For the same reasons we've just talked about—if they do things right, well, that's what they're supposed to do. Why get excited when people do what they're supposed to do, right? Well, there are probably a million reasons why we should focus on the positives in people, but for the sake of time, here are a few. Pointing out the positive in people…

➢ makes them feel good
➢ makes them feel appreciated
➢ builds their self-esteem
➢ builds their confidence
➢ gives them incentive
➢ provides motivation
➢ helps them focus on the positive as well
➢ builds morale

How do you feel when someone points out the positive in you? Enough said.

Now, let's look at giving credit for a team accomplishment. Let's say your group finishes a project ahead of time, comes in under budget, or discovers a new way of doing something. Who gets the credit? What if it was one person in particular? What if it was a small team within your larger group? Let's go further. What if you were being interviewed by the media— to whom would you give credit? What if you were standing before your board of directors—to whom would you give credit?

A good leader shares the credit when something goes right. Better yet, a good leader *gives* the credit. I know this is the exact opposite of what we said in the last chapter about leaders assuming responsibility when something goes wrong. Think of responsibility and credit as a give and take—leaders *take* responsibility and they *give* credit.

As humans we tend to want to take the credit when things go right. It's natural to want to look good or important to the world. Rather, this is an opportunity to experience growth toward leadership. Remember, leadership is not about you; it's about others; it's about the group; and it's about relationships. Leadership is not about your goals, it's about the team's goals. If you take the credit for something accomplished by your team, how will the people on your team feel? How will they view you? What will it do to your relationships? Worse yet, how will it affect the trust between you and your team?

If you want to make yourself look good, then make others look good. Share the credit by using "we" instead of "I" or "me." Give the credit where credit is due. If a particular person or group is responsible for the accomplishment, then don't hold back, give them the credit. By giving credit where credit is due, you'll strengthen the connection with your team by building trust and goodwill.

People need to feel important and worthwhile. Acknowledging their positives gives them the fuel needed to continue to perform. People need motivation; they need encouragement; and they need recognition.

If you take the credit without recognizing the person to whom it's due, you not only will lose trust, but it can create resentment toward you. That's a sure-fire way to demotivate the people on your team. Would you want to work for a person or organization that you resented? Would you give 100 percent effort, or would you do the bare minimum?

Many people want to succeed; they want to give 110 percent; and they want to go the extra mile. As a leader, you've got to give them a reason or motivation to do so. Otherwise, you have people who are just going through the motions. How much more effective could your team, group, or organization be if all your employees and volunteers were giving 110 percent?

Recognizing people for their positive contributions doesn't have to be extravagant or expensive. Neither does recognition have to be in the form of monetary compensation. Here are a few ideas to give recognition to the people on your team. Some are more reserved and some are a little cheesy. Try them anyway, you'll be surprised how good it will make people feel.

- Start looking for the positives, even if they're small.
- Call the person in your office to let them know how much you appreciate their efforts. Or even better, take the time to go to their desk or office to let them know how much you appreciate their efforts.
- Buy doughnuts or cookies and write a short note on the outside of the box. "Thank you, Susan!" "Well done, Mike!" "Way to go, Susan, Mike, and Terry!"
- Buy one of those big cupcakes and place it on their desk before they get to work. Write a note of appreciation on the box.
- Take the team out to lunch or for drinks after work.
- Order pizza or catering and have it delivered to the office.

- Send a handwritten note to the person's home. Sure you could just hand it to them at work, but writing the note and mailing it to their home demonstrates that you took the time to show you care.
- Give the person a small gift card to their favorite restaurant or coffee shop.
- Ask if they'd like additional responsibility or a special project. If they want more, give them the opportunity to do more. Let them know they've earned it. (Seems a little counterintuitive to earn the right to do more work, but some people are actually looking for growth and advancement.)
- Give a coupon to leave work an hour earlier on Friday. When they turn it in, don't give them a hard time about it, that will negate the purpose.

When it comes to recognition, think equal-opportunity. Spread your recognition around. Look for ways to include everyone when possible. When people see others being recognized, it sparks a flame of desire to be recognized as well. Surely, everyone does something positive once in a while, right?

In summary, to build better connections with your team:

- Look for the positives—We often overlook the positive things people do because we think that's what they should do. However, we'll point out the negative because, even though very little goes as planned, we're somehow surprised when things go wrong. Be conscious of this human tendency and look for the positives.
- Feed the positive—Focus on the negative and you'll see more negative; focus on the positive and you'll see more positive.
- Create buffers for the unplanned—Things happen, things cost more than expected, and things take longer than expected. Add a little extra time and cost to your planning as a buffer. When unplanned things happen, assess what went right and what went wrong, then make adjustments for the future.
- Point out the positive things people do—Showing recognition for the positive things people do makes them feel good, appreciated, and encouraged.
- Give credit where credit is due—Leaders give the credit to the team and to the individuals responsible for the win. Leaders take responsibility and give credit.

Questions for Growth

1. How would you describe yourself when it comes to focusing on the negatives and positives that happen in the normal course of life? In others? In yourself?

2. Do you get frustrated when things don't go as planned?
3. How can you better plan for the unexpected?
4. Would you agree that when things go right, we don't get excited because we have a tendency to think that's the way it should be?
5. What can you do to acknowledge when things go right in your personal life?
6. What can you do to acknowledge when things go right at work?
7. How do you feel about giving the credit where credit is due?
8. What can you do to show your appreciation, encouragement, or acknowledgement to those around you, even when it's something you feel they should be doing anyway?

26

LEADERS ARE SOLUTION-ORIENTED

A big part of a leader's responsibility is to solve problems, in other words, to be solution-oriented. Again, it's important to note that you don't have to be the person in-charge to exhibit leadership abilities. The following example demonstrates how anyone, even in an entry-level position, can be solution-oriented. Let me tell you about Rachel.

I absolutely must have my morning coffee or else I'm sure I'll die. I woke up one Saturday morning at my usual 5:30 a.m. It was cold and rainy outside. Sleeping in would've been nice, but I'm an early riser and can't sleep late. I went straight to the kitchen to turn on the coffee maker. Nothing happened. I unplugged it and plugged it back in; still nothing. The power wasn't out because the lights on the other appliances were on. The coffee maker must've bit the dust. I began to panic.

I recalled an el-cheapo coffee maker we'd received as a wedding gift. The last time I saw it was in the attic. I didn't want to wake my wife so I slowly pulled down the attic door, climbed the creaking ladder, and searched the attic as best I could. The coffee pot wasn't there. As I climbed down the ladder I remembered a wedding we attended a few months earlier, and I'm almost certain we re-gifted the coffee maker to those folks. (It's okay to re-gift. Just make sure they're not the ones who gave it to you in the first place.)

It was now 5:45 on a cold, rainy Saturday morning…and no coffee.

I had no choice but to get dressed, throw on a baseball hat, and drive to the Starbucks about a mile from the house. When I got there I jumped out of the car and ran through the rain to the door. The door was locked! After a few minutes the young lady working that morning opened the door, greeted me with a smile, and a "Good morning!" Well, I didn't say it out loud, but it actually wasn't such a good morning so far. I was impressed, however, with her positive attitude on such a dreary day.

I walked to the counter to order, "Yes, I'll have a grande dark roast, please."

"Sir, we don't have any coffee," she replied.

"You don't have any coffee! This early in the morning? This is Starbucks, isn't it?" At first I thought she was joking, but she wasn't. At this point I almost lost it. A coffee shop with no coffee? Was this a practical joke? Was I being Punk'd?

Apparently, a severe thunderstorm caused a fuse to blow in the coffee machines.

Suddenly I became concerned for this young lady. According to her name tag, her name was Rachel.

"Rachel, what are you gonna do? You're about to be bombarded with a boatload of angry customers."

Rachel looked a little panicked, but assured me she'd already called her manager and the manager had called the repair person. I wished her good luck and headed toward the door.

Just as I opened the door to leave, Rachel said, "Sir, wait!"

Rachel came running from around the counter and picked up a box from the retail display. She opened the box and pulled out a French press. "Sir, our coffee machines may be broke, but we have hot water. If you'll give me five minutes, I'll make you some coffee with this French press. Some people say it's even better than our drip coffee."

I needed coffee, so I was game.

For the next hour, Rachel made French press coffee for every customer that walked in out of the cold, that is, until the manager showed up at 7 a.m.

The manager rushed in and saw several opened French press boxes and the French presses lined up on the counter. The manager was furious. "What in the world are you doing with all these French presses? You can't open all these boxes. Who's gonna pay for them? Did you at least charge for the coffee you made? What in the world were you thinking?"

Rachel's reply made a lasting impression on me. She said, "I didn't have time to worry about that. I was just trying to make the customers some coffee."

After overhearing the exchange between the manager and Rachel, I went up to the counter and said, "Rachel, you were right, I think this coffee is better than the drip coffee. Can I buy one of those French presses?"

Rachel responded, "Sure, let me get you a new one off the shelf."

I said, "No, no, I'd like one of these you've already opened if that's okay."

Then, several other customers followed until we bought all the French presses Rachel had opened.

Rachel could've charged me for the French press coffee, but she didn't.

She was busy making coffee by hand and focusing on the customers as they walked in the door. She could've sent me away to find coffee elsewhere, but she didn't. She was resourceful and figured out a way to serve her customers in spite of a major obstacle.

To solve the problem, Rachel took a risk. I'm not sure that she actually calculated the cost of opening three or four French press boxes, but assuming they were only $12 each, then she could've easily paid for it if she had to. Rachel's small risk paid off. Not only did she sell the French presses she opened, but she made a handful of regular customers very, I mean *very*, happy.

In short, Rachel turned an awful experience into an awesome experience.

A few years later I read a book about Starbucks and came across the quote (mentioned earlier in chapter 23) from Howard Shultz, the company's founder and CEO. Here's the quote:

"We are not in the coffee business serving people,
we are in the people business serving coffee."

After reading that I think Mr. Shultz would've approved of Rachel's actions.

Rachel wasn't the manager; she wasn't even a barista. Rachel was a cashier. She definitely was not in a leadership role. Yet, she made a decision on her own. In my opinion, what made Rachel's decision effective was that it was focused on the right thing—serving the customers. I believe she saw her job as more than taking customer's orders and getting their money; she was there to serve the customers first and foremost.

As a side note, Rachel was the only customer service person at that Starbucks location who wore a name tag. All the workers wore an employee lanyard with an ID card, but it was hard to see their names because, most of the time, the lanyard was either spinning or turned backward. In addition to the lanyard Rachel had her own name tag. It was a generic name tag that simply said, "Rachel." I asked her about it one day and she said it was her name tag at a previous job. "I'm just curious, why do you wear it?" I asked. She said, "Well, I see your name every day when you hand me your credit card. It's only fair that I wear a name tag so we can learn each other's name."

Rachel got it. She knew how to connect with people and she did a dang good job of doing it.

Bottom-line: You don't have to be *the* leader to be *a* leader.

Questions for Growth

1. Would you consider yourself to be solution-oriented?
2. If you're not the leader, would you feel comfortable making a decision to solve an immediate problem? Why or why not?

3. If you are the leader, do you give leeway to lower-level participants to make decisions, or must they check with you first?
4. What types of decisions are allowed?
5. What types of decisions are not allowed?
6. What risks are involved in allowing lower-level participants to make decisions?
7. What benefits are there in allowing lower-level participants to make decisions?
8. What improvements could be made to allow participants, at all levels, to make solution-oriented decisions?

27

DEALING WITH CHANGE

Few people like change; some people, however, crave change. Some people think change is awful; others think change is great. Some feel change is negative; others feel change is progress. Some people avoid change; others welcome change.

Whichever side you're on, it's important to understand how to cope with change, as well as how to help others deal with change.

There was a story I heard many years ago about a young pastor who was recently hired at a church. The church had been around for almost a hundred years. The last pastor retired after serving the church for 30 years. Many of the members grew up in the church and had been going there for many decades.

The new, young pastor was a good preacher and people person. The congregation loved him. He felt he had some great ideas to help the church grow.

On his first Sunday as pastor he moved the podium from the side of the pulpit (stage) to the center. He didn't understand why the podium was placed to one side and felt he could see and connect better with the entire congregation with the podium in the center.

Moods changed immediately. The congregation didn't like the fact that the new pastor moved the podium from the side to the center of the pulpit. The podium has always been offset to the side of the pulpit. Within three months he was asked to resign. The young pastor and his family accepted the fate and moved away.

A few years later the young pastor happened to be traveling through this town where he served such a short time. He decided to visit the church that Sunday morning to see how things were going. He sat in the back so he could observe from a good vantage point.

Immediately he noticed that the podium was in the middle of the pulpit.

He was shocked, as he should be, since that was the reason he was basically fired. This bothered him so much that he could hardly pay attention to the sermon.

After the service he waited around until most of the congregation had left. He introduced himself to the current pastor and explained what happened to him a few years ago. He said, "You see, when I was hired I moved the podium from the side of the pulpit to the center and within three months of being hired, I was asked to leave. How in the world is it that *you* have been able to move the pulpit to the center? I just don't get it."

The current pastor replied, "I heard what happened to you, and I agreed with you that the podium should be in the center, not off to one side."

"So how'd you do it?" the previous pastor asked.

"I moved it one inch per week and they never even noticed."

Often people are resistant to change. But in reality it seems to be the *rate of change* that is the problem. In general, the greater the rate of change, the greater the stress created by those affected. Slow change or smaller changes over time are more acceptable than immediate or larger changes. However, in some cases the changes can't be made slowly or in smaller increments, such as when there's an immediate change in management. Learning how to cope with change yourself, as well as helping others cope with change, is an important skill for leaders to learn.

Change is a fact. As long as there have been people on this earth there has been change. It seems as though the rate of change has been increasing rapidly over the past century. Look at technology! What would Alexander Graham Bell say if he heard a kid say, "Hey Dad, can I play your phone?" And look at travel in the past hundred or so years. We've gone from horse and buggy to cars to planes and to space travel. Change is here to stay.

Let's look at some ways to help make change more palatable.

If you're the one implementing change:

- ➤ One of the first questions to ask is, "How can we implement this change in the least disruptive way?" You can't always accomplish this, but if it's possible, then at least consider a manner of delivery that will be more palatable.
- ➤ Be understanding of those who are affected by the change. Change causes people to have certain feelings such as fear and anxiety. Be sensitive to these feelings. Acknowledge peoples' fears and allow them to express them without judgement or denial. Don't just tell them to deal with it; help them to deal with it.
- ➤ When possible, get buy-in from all those involved; don't just spring it on them. Even presidential candidates get buy-in from their

supporters. Getting buy-in doesn't necessarily mean 100 percent agreement. It means to discuss the problem, the need for change, and the possible alternatives. When people feel involved in the process, they are more likely to accept and support the change rather than fight it. Besides, there may be something you don't know that only someone working on the front lines can tell you. This information can be valuable to developing and implementing plans of change.

➤ Communicate, communicate, communicate. Explain what's going on so people will know what to expect, even if you don't know what the future holds. Be straightforward, but understanding. Allow people to talk and express their feelings without fear of backlash. Open communication creates transparency and authenticity.

➤ Put people first. Yes, the change may be important and necessary, but so are the people affected by the change. How you handle the situation will communicate what's more important to you and the organization: the *change* or the *people* involved in the change. Your people can help or hinder the change, but it depends on how you treat them in the process.

➤ Implement change gradually when possible. Small changes are more acceptable than sweeping changes. There was a tax preparer who needed to increase her average fee by about $50. Rather than raising the fee all at once, the accountant discussed the increase with her clients and increased the fee by $10 per year. All of the clients stayed and supported the gradual fee increase.

If the change is happening to you:

➤ Respectfully ask for clarification. Rather than automatically opposing the change, ask for more information. I emphasize *respectfully,* and should perhaps add *sincerely,* because sometimes people have a tendency to lash out, criticize, or blame in reaction to an event, such as change, particularly when it affects them directly.

➤ Ask how you can help and be a part of the process.

➤ Help others deal with the change. Your leadership among co-participants (your peers) can help them process the change, mentally and physically.

➤ Communicate in a positive way with your peers. Don't get involved in negative talk, it will only make the situation worse.

➤ Be willing to develop new skills that might be needed as a result of the change. Those who are willing to adapt are more likely to overcome the stress caused by change.

> ➤ Much of the anxiety caused by change is a fear of the unknown or an uncertainty of what lies ahead. This feeling leads to insecurity, particular of one's employment. It's natural to enjoy our comfort zone. Even if our comfort zone is not ideal, at least we know what to expect. Sometimes the situation is bleak, like when a manufacturing plant closes and many people lose their job. What can you do? Move forward; investigate your possibilities; consider all avenues. I know a man who lost his job at a manufacturing plant. He and several co-workers looked at the possibilities and a few decided to go to mortuary school. He later became coroner in Dougherty County, Georgia. I met Michael Fowler, Sr. in my Rotary Club and his story inspired me. I hope it inspires you as well, not necessarily to become a mortician, but to explore all your possibilities.

Change is one of those things that makes us feel out of control. And that's usually true; change is usually imposed upon us. We can fight it, but most of the time the attempt is futile. If there's one thing I can guarantee you it is this: *change is coming*. Change has always been with us and will stay with us.

Here are a few quotes that help me deal with change:

If you're coasting, you're going downhill.

There is no standing still, you're either moving forward or falling behind.

Blessed are the flexible for they shall not get bent out of shape.

Leaders are constantly looking for personal growth. They're continual learners, in skill and knowledge. This continual improvement helps to be prepared in times of change. There's a great book, an easy read, that I highly recommend, *Who Moved My Cheese?* by Spencer Johnson and Kenneth Blanchard. The book illustrates how people respond differently to change. The point is to never assume your cheese will always be there, but to always be looking for new cheese. At some point your cheese *will* move.

Questions for Growth

1. How do you feel about change?
2. Can you describe a situation where change impacted you directly?
3. How do you feel about getting outside your comfort zone?
4. Do you feel that change is always bad?
5. How can change be positive?
6. How do you feel about gradual change?

7. How do you feel about sudden change?
8. Have you read the book, *Who Moved My Cheese?* By Spencer
    Johnson and Kenneth Blanchard? If not, would you consider
    reading it?

Recommended Reading:
Who Moved My Cheese?: An Amazing Way to Deal with Change in Your Work and in Your Life by
Spencer Johnson, M.D. and Kenneth Blanchard.

28

CREATE A PATH

My family and I were traveling down a two-lane, country highway. Tall trees and brush bordered both sides of the road. When we got to this one stretch of highway we noticed a construction crew with large equipment cutting down trees to widen the road from a two-lane to a four-lane. My son, who was about eight at the time, said, "It looks like they're creating a path."

I said, "I think you're right."

He then said, "I saw this on my tractor video. They are making the way so the pavers can come in to build the road."

The more I thought about what he said, the more I realized it was a pretty cool analogy about how leaders create a path for the team to do the work necessary to pursue the desire outcome.

How do leaders create a path? Although there are many concepts that could be considered part of the means by which leaders create a path, I've boiled it down to three that are practical for both small and large organizations and can be implemented immediately.

Create a Vision

The first step to creating a path is to create a vision. Now, you may be thinking that creating a vision is one of those lofty, big picture plans that only great visionaries can do. Bill Gates (Microsoft) and Steve Jobs (Apple) come to mind. But we can't leave out Sam Walton (Walmart), Ray Kroc (McDonald's), or Howard Shultz (Starbucks). All of these were great visionaries who developed great companies. But creating a vision is not just for these pioneers.

Creating a vision is for you, too. Whether you are a team leader, division manager, or any other leader, creating a vision is just as important for you. Maybe you haven't thought about it as creating a vision, but you may very well be doing this already to some extent. Let's say your team is assigned a project. How do you see this project coming to life, unfolding, and being completed? These questions are exactly what it takes to create a vision to accomplish the project.

Sometimes, if not often, we may bypass the vision process and get right down to work. In certain situations that may be fine. But what if a little more thought or vision went into the planning before work begins? Could it be done better, for example, more efficiently, faster, or at a lower cost? What is the decision process? How will problems be solved? How will a positive environment be developed and maintained for all participants? What will motivation look like? How will morale be lifted?

Every situation (that I can imagine) can use a vision. Consider your family vacations. Your vacation planning starts with a vision. Perhaps you or your spouse come up with a vacation idea, "You know, I'd kind of like to go to the mountains this year." Now that may sound like a simple destination, but it's really more than that. What was being pictured as the thought of the mountains came to mind? Why would the mountains be a good vacation? Would going to the mountains solve an issue the family is currently facing? What activities would be enjoyable for the family? What feelings are generated from imagining a family vacation in the mountains? How do you see the family bonding during the trip? All of these questions are part of the vision.

Out of curiosity, have you ever had a vision of doing something with your family and you picture something where everyone gets along, the kids have an emotional experience, and your family truly appreciates the time spent together? How did it really turn out? Rarely does it turn out the way you imagined. Just because you have a vision doesn't mean anyone else has the same vision. One of the best ways to improve the chances of your vision coming to life is to communicate it to the others in your family. You might start with writing it down for yourself. Then, at each point along the way share a story or a memory to help them better understand why this particular place or activity means so much to you. I know my kids love to hear stories from my childhood.

A vision works the same way in your organization. Start by writing it down. A vision does not have to be a 700-page novel. Ideally, your vision should fit on one page. It should be simple and easy to communicate. And, the vision must be crystal clear. Then, communicate, communicate, communicate. Share stories, analogies, and inspirations to help your team better understand the why's and how's of your vision.

There's a verse in the Bible applicable to the need for creating and sharing your vision:

Where there is no vision, the people perish. Proverbs 29:18 (King James Version)

Systems and Processes

Another way to create a path is to develop systems and processes for all to follow.

I once visited a women's clothing boutique to buy my wife a gift card for her birthday. There were two young ladies, I would say teenagers, standing behind the counter. One appeared to be the trainer and the other the trainee. The trainer asked, "Can I help you?"

"Yes, I'd like a $50 gift card for my wife's birthday."

Without saying anything to me, the trainer turned to the trainee and said, "See that notebook. That's for gift cards. Hand me the notebook and I'll show you how to do gift cards."

The trainee handed her the notebook. Then the trainer began to explain how to do gift cards. She said, "First, you open the notebook to the first page. Then you find the last gift card number on the list. If the number was 243, then the next gift certificate should be number 244. The gift certificates are in the back of the notebook. Turn to the back of the notebook, unzip the pouch, and get the next gift certificate on top. Make sure it is number 244. Then flip back to the first page. Get a pen from over there. Write down the gift certificate number in the first column. Write today's date in the second column. Write the customer's name in the third column and who they're buying it for in the fourth column. In the last column write the amount of the gift certificate."

The trainee started filling out the gift certificate chart. When she got to the customer's name, she whispered to the trainer, "What's the customer's name?"

The trainer looked up at me and asked, "What's your name?"

I said, "Bil Sadler," and thinking I'd help them out to speed up the process, I added, "and I'm buying it for Heather Sadler."

The trainer then narrated, to the trainee, each item as the trainee wrote in the chart. "Write the gift certificate number, then the customer's name, then the person it's for, and then the amount."

I thought we were home free when the chart was completed. Nope.

The trainer then gave further instructions to the trainee, "Close the notebook and put it back over there. Open the cash register and there's a piece of paper under the drawer. You've got to write down the gift certificate information on this piece of paper and leave it in the drawer. Then you ask how they want to pay for it."

The trainer looked up at me and asked, "How would you like to pay for it?"

"Credit card," I responded.

Again, without saying anything to me, the trainer says to the trainee, "If they're paying by credit card, you need to make a note of it on this piece of paper. Just put CC out to the right."

The trainer processed my credit card and then asked, "Would you like this gift wrapped?"

"Sure, why not."

The trainer then went through another long, step-by-step, instruction on how to gift wrap a gift card.

This was one of the most painful transactions I've ever experienced. After one of them handed me my gift wrapped gift certificate, I asked, "I'm just curious, do you have that process written down anywhere?"

The trainer said, "No, we just go over a few times until they learn it."

All I could say was, "I see."

Now, I know that buying a gift certificate should be a fairly simple thing, but even a simple thing can have a complicated process. How much easier would it have been if the trainer in the above scenario could've simply told the trainee to follow the steps in the training manual? The trainee could've opened the training manual to the page for "Gift Cards" and followed the steps. Simple, right?

The problem with creating a step-by-step process for any given routine is that it takes time to create. Yes, it does take time to write down the steps. However, it can save tons of time once it's written. Not only will it aid in training, but it will help experienced employees as well. If there's a task you don't do frequently, it's easy to forget how to do the task—look at the written process and there's no need to memorize it. If a manager has to be called to help with the task, then the labor cost is increased and productivity is reduced—just look at the written process. If an experienced person quits without much notice, their knowledge and experience walks out the door, too. How do you train their replacement in a cost-effective and time-efficient manner? Simple, use a written process.

Yes, a written process takes time to create, but consider it an investment that pays huge dividends in the future. Create a written process for every task, routine and infrequent, in your organization. Even the simple ones.

But that's micromanaging, isn't it? No, it actually keeps you from micromanaging. If there's a process to follow, why should you be involved?

How can I as the leader create a process for every activity in my organization? *You* don't. Let the person doing the task create the process. They're closer to it and probably know how to do it better than you anyway.

How do I know the processes are complete and accurate? Periodically have someone, other than the creator, do the task using the written process. They must follow the process only and cannot receive help from the person who created the process. The process must be thorough with nothing left to the imagination. No matter how simple or self-explanatory a step might be, write it down as part of the process.

The more routine the task, the more need for a written process.

Approvals, purchase orders, resource requisitions, customer contact, customer service, product development, production, just to name a few, typically involve a process. Routine tasks can create bottleneck problems if a person quits. A written process will help make a smooth transition when training new employees.

These written processes provide guidance to the participants doing the work, improve efficiency and productivity, and reduce labor costs in the long-run.

Here's one last example of a process I use in my personal life that can easily be applied to a work situation. Back in the 1990s I worked for a public accounting firm. Many of the firm's clients were out-of-town and the work often required overnight travel. One of the partners I worked for shared an idea that I still use today. First, he told me to buy a men's toiletry bag and a second set of everything that goes in it, such as a razor, toothbrush, toothpaste, shampoo, soap, and so on. Before this idea I was looking around the bathroom trying to remember what all I needed to take with me. Second, he showed me his travel checklist. It was a list of every possible thing he needed for the trip. It included obvious things like underwear, undershirts, suits, socks, shoes, and anything else you can think of. Not all things were necessary on every trip, like a swimsuit, but at least it was on the list to consider. The benefit of using this travel list and grabbing the ready-to-go toiletry bag is that I can pack in ten minutes flat, if that. Oh, and there's one more benefit—I no longer have that feeling that I forgot something.

Want things to go right more often? Create a written process for all activities and tasks.

Provide Clarity

Remember the lines from *Alice in Wonderland* (Lewis Carroll) where Alice asks the Cheshire Cat, "Would you tell me, please, which way I ought to go from here?"

The Cheshire Cat says, "That depends a good deal on where you want to get to."

Alice says, "I don't much care where."

Then the Cheshire Cat replies, "Then it doesn't matter which way you go."

"So long as I get *somewhere,*" Alice added.

"Oh, you're sure to do that," said the Cat, "if you only walk long enough."

I love this exchange between the Cheshire Cat and Alice! It's the perfect example of how some people go about living their lives. They don't know where they're going; they take the path of least resistance; and they wait for opportunities to find them. Many people are in their current job because of this very reason. They needed money, a job was available, so they applied and got the job. The job isn't special and has no meaning; it's just a job. They go to work, do their job, and repeat the process the next day. They're doing what they're doing because the opportunity arose and, for some reason, they acted upon it. This common scenario happens because it lacks clarity. Without clarity, it doesn't matter which way you go. But if you keep walking long enough, you're sure to end up somewhere.

If you ask most people where they are going, what will they say? Do they know where they're going? Do you know where you're going? Clarity will help answer this question.

Let's say you and your family want to go to the beach for summer vacation. You ask your spouse which beach? He or she says, "Oh, it doesn't really matter as long as we go to the beach?" Does this answer make your planning easier or more difficult? What if your spouse says, "I'd like to go to Destin, Florida the second week of June." Does this answer simplify your planning? It should. Your planning will be more time-efficient because you'll know exactly where (Destin) and when (second week of June) to look for a place to stay.

Clarity provides direction. When someone is clear on the direction, getting there is much easier. Clarity improves efficiency, effectiveness, and performance.

When you create a path, whether it's a vision or a process, provide as much clarity as you can. Clarity comes from simplicity, clear descriptions, and conciseness. Clarity increases the probability of success. When possible, don't leave performance to chance, provide clarity.

Questions for Growth

1. Do you ever feel like where you're headed is some vague place, and you're not sure you'll even know when you've arrived?
2. Conversely, have you ever felt like you knew exactly where you are going and what you need to do to get there?
3. How do you articulate a clear vision with those you lead?
4. How could you improve on creating clarity with those you lead?
5. How would you describe any processes or systems you have in place?
6. Are there other processes or systems that could be created in your work (or at home)?
7. How could the travel list and toiletry bag idea help make your packing more efficient? How could it help mentally?
8. How could the travel list idea apply to other situations?

29

ENCOURAGE AND EMPOWER

When I was around 10-years old my dad starting teaching me how to mow the grass. By the time I was 12 I was able to mow our lawn on my own. Dad paid me $5 each time I mowed the lawn—that was big money back then! One day it hit me that I could make some serious money if I could start cutting grass for the neighbors. I mentioned it to Dad and he agreed, "Why don't you start with the neighbors across the street, Mr. and Mrs. Stover?"

I said, "They already have two high school boys from down the street to cut their grass. Besides, I'm only 12 and they're much bigger than I am."

Dad said, "Son, you never know. Why don't you at least let the Stovers know you'd be interested if the opportunity opens up?"

So I did. Mr. Stover said exactly what I thought he'd say, "I have some high school boys cut my grass. Maybe when you get a little bigger."

I was discouraged.

Dad asked me how it went and I told him. Dad said, "Son, look, you may only be 12-years old, but you mow our lawn all by yourself and you do a great job. Hang in there, you'll get the opportunity."

About a year later, that opportunity came. Those two high school boys cut the Stover's yard. I don't know what kind of equipment they used to mow it, but they butchered it. That was the worst lawn mowing job I had ever seen! I told Dad about it and he said, "Well, this may be your opportunity. Make a point to talk to Mr. Stover and offer to fix it."

That afternoon I waited in my front yard for Mr. Stover to come home from work. He stepped out of his car, put his hands on his hips, and his face turned red—to put it mildly, he was ticked off. He looked over at me across the street and said in a gruff voice, "Did you do this to my yard?"

I walked across the street to stand in front of Mr. Stover and said, "No sir, it was the two high school boys who always cut your yard. I mow our lawn all the time. If you'd like, I can fix it for you right now."

And that's how I got my first lawn mowing customer. It was through my dad's encouragement that helped me learn how to push a lawn mower, how to cut around trees and shrubs, and how to mow in straight lines. He also encouraged me to ask. When I got a "No," he encouraged me to hang in there until the opportunity came open.

People need encouragement. It gives them hope, confidence, and assurance. People need to know that someone believes in them.

When you encourage someone, it draws them closer to you. It strengthens your connection and deepens your relationship. Try it. Try it at home and try it at work. This is what good leaders do, they encourage others.

Good leaders also empower others. In the above example, Dad empowered me to mow the lawn. He taught me in great detail how to do it, then he let me do it. I didn't know any other kids my age who were able to mow the grass. Sure I made mistakes every now and then, but Dad helped me work through them. One time I ran over a root and damaged the mower. I thought Dad was going to kill me, but he didn't. He got the mower fixed and showed me how to mow over and around roots. He could've taken the job away from me, but he didn't. He empowered me to handle it.

People will make mistakes. People also learn from their mistakes; don't give up on them. Rather than chastising them for their mistakes, be a coach. Treat this as a training opportunity. Ask for their assessment of the situation and ideas for improvement. Provide guidance as needed, and encouragement always.

Mr. Stover also empowered me. I'm sure he was very reluctant to let a 12- or 13-year old cut the grass when most other kids cutting grass were in high school. But he did. Mr. Stover empowered me to fix the mistake made by the two high school boys. At the time, I had no idea what empowerment was, but I know I felt it. It made me want to do a good job, no, a great job. I took my time mowing his lawn and when I got finished it looked like a putting green. I was proud of my work. And Mr. Stover was happy as well.

When you empower someone, you fuel a desire within them to do a great job. The task becomes theirs; they take responsibility; it gives them opportunity. When someone owns the task, they take pride in doing it right. Rather than doing something for you, they're doing it for themselves.

Instead of micromanaging someone, try giving them space and freedom to handle it. Imagine you're a coach. A coach provides instructions, training, and feedback. Then the coach lets the players play the game. A good coach empowers the players to do their job. In return the players give it their all.

Even though empowering someone to do something on their own may seem like you're creating a separation between you and them, it's actually strengthening your connection. Why? One word—trust. Empowering someone is putting your trust in them. How do you feel when you know that someone trusts you?

If you have a team or you're on a team, you can build and strengthen your connections by encouraging and empowering others. You don't have to be the leader-in-charge to be an encourager—you can lead by example from any position.

Encourage and empower others.

Questions for Growth

1. Think of a time when someone encouraged or empowered you. Describe the situation and how you felt.
2. Think of a time when you've encouraged or empowered someone else. Describe the situation, how you felt, and how you think the other person felt.
3. Are there people around you who need your encouragement right now?
4. Are there people who need your empowerment so they can do their thing (or job)?
5. How do you feel about giving encouragement?
6. How do you feel about letting go and empowering others?
7. Do you have room for improvement in your encouragement and empowerment of others?

30

CHARACTER

Your character is the all-encompassing total of everything that makes you who you are today. It's how you see yourself and how others see you. It's the way you look, the way you think, the things you believe, your morals, your values, your experiences, your reputation, your qualities, and even your peculiarities. It's everything about you. Your character is not the same as your personality, although your character may influence your personality.

The "way you are" is shaped by the people in your life and your past experiences. The people in your life may have been encouraging, or they may have been hurtful. Your past experiences may include some triumphs, but it could also include some adversity. Both the joys and the pains had a part in shaping your character.

Often when we think of character we think of honesty, integrity, and trustworthiness. We may say a person is of good character if these qualities are demonstrated consistently, even when no one is looking. For example, if you paid for an item and received too much change from the cashier, you either look at it like it was your lucky day, or you return the money. If you return the money someone might say you are of good character. Your character includes your degree, whether low or high, of honesty, integrity, and trustworthiness.

Your character also includes your level of self-discipline, confidence, determination, personal responsibility, willingness to work with others (sociability), ability to cope with change (flexibility), desire for personal growth, and desire to help and serve others, to name a few traits.

Although your character is developed from everything that's happened to you in the past, it helps you form views and make choices about your future. Because you have the ability to make choices, I believe that everyone, including you and me, has the capability of improving our character. When we make a positive decision, our character is improved.

When we make a negative decision, our character is lessened. It is with each choice you make that your character is shaped. Although one positive choice won't change your character overnight, it will immediately change the *direction* of your character.

If you desire to change the direction of your character, I believe you can do so starting right now. It all starts with your desire. If you have the desire, then make the decision that you *will* change the direction of your character. Don't worry about the how's and why's at this point, just have the desire and make the decision.

Next, you absolutely must believe in yourself. Whether anyone else believes in you or not, believe in yourself. If you've heard negative stuff in your past, use it to your advantage. That's right, use it. If I asked you to forget all the negative stuff, could you? That's like saying, "Don't picture a purple elephant." What will you do? You'll picture a purple elephant. Rather than forget the negativity, use it as fuel for personal growth.

In January 1974 we moved to a new town right in the middle of my first grade year. One day at my new school I remember the teacher dividing the class into reading groups. The groups were divided based on reading ability. For some reason my teacher made a point to tell me that I couldn't be in the top reading group, and she said it in front of the entire class. I didn't like hearing that. I may have misunderstood what she really meant, but I've always felt like it was a negative, hurtful comment. That experience could've labeled me for the rest of my life, but I guess I had some of my dad's determination and *oh-yeah, well-I'll-show-you* trait. My mom helped me with my reading and by the second grade I was in the top reading group.

Negativity hurts, but you can use it for fuel to become better. Believe in yourself.

Next, make choices that propel you in the right direction. Your ability to make choices is one of the most powerful gifts you've been given as a human. Sure, you can blame how and where you were raised, you can point to the terrible things that happened to you in the past, and you can blame specific people if you'd like. But the bottom line is that the very next choice is yours to make. Will your choice be tainted by the things you blame or where you're from, or will your choice transcend you to where you want to go? It really is your choice.

Often we think of making choices in random situations that require us to make a decision. A random situation is one that presents itself outside of your control. It's as if you're just walking along and all of a sudden you come to a fork in the road. You didn't know the fork was coming, it just presented itself. Which choice will you make? That's one type of choice, the kind that arises outside of your control. There's another type of choice that comes from within you. I'll put it like this: *You don't have to wait for choices to arise. Make your own choices.* One choice can change the direction of life.

Here's an analogy that illustrates the difference in waiting for things to happen versus making things happen. In sales, there are generally two types of salespeople, order-takers and order-makers. Order-takers wait for a customer to walk up to the counter, they wait for the phone to ring, or they wait for an email to show up in their inbox. In other words, order-takers wait for business to happen to them.

By contrast, order-makers don't wait around for prospects to show up. Order-makers go hunting for prospects. They put themselves out there in front of people; they create conversations out of thin air; and they look for opportunities to serve. Order-makers generate business from their own efforts. It is their choice.

If you want to improve your character, start with your next choice.

Connecting

Your character also affects your relationships through your influence and example. How are you toward others? Do you have a concern for others? A desire to serve? Are you kind and compassionate? Do you encourage others? Do you listen? Do you work well with others? Are you flexible? All of the ways you are toward others determine your ability to connect. Connections build relationships, one small connection at a time.

There's a saying in the sales industry called the ABC's—*Always Be Closing*. If you're in sales then you get it. Although this sounds logical, I challenge it. Here's why. Closing is about you, not your customer. And if it's about you, how are you connecting? The justification I hear is that when you close a sale you're helping the customer's situation with your product or service. If it truly does help then I can't argue with that. My argument, however, is not about closing, it's about *always* closing. Have you ever had a salesperson start closing with your first inquiry? My mom was looking at vehicle a few years ago and she simply asked a question about the color. The salesperson said, "If we can get it in silver, will you be ready to drive it home today?" My mom said, "I don't know about that, I just asked if you can get it in silver. So can you or can you not?" (I couldn't have said it better myself. Go mom!)

Rather than ABC meaning *Always Be Closing*, I like to say ABC stands for *Always Be Connecting*. Is your character one of *connecting*? If not, it can be. Connecting does not have to be something grandiose. It's the small things that are focused toward others. It's putting others first. It's putting your team's goals ahead of your goals.

If you really want a challenge, try to connect with someone who has a different opinion or view than yours. First of all, it's okay for people to have different opinions. Second, take the pressure off yourself—you don't have to convince everyone to see it your way. Other than you, who says your way is the right way? Remember in chapter 11 when we talked about listening to understand? Try that. I know it sounds easy, but it's not. On the other hand, it may be easier to listen-to-understand than it is to try to convince someone that their view is wrong. The hard part is for you to stop thinking it's your duty to make people see everything your way. Give it up. It ain't gonna work anyway.

Unity

Another aspect of character that is often misunderstood is a leader's ability to connect *others* together. In other words, does the leader create unity among all, or does the leader create division among groups. This is most obvious in the political realm, mainly through critical remarks, even name calling, against anyone who has a different view. These comments are quite divisive in nature. However, there are some, maybe a few, political leaders who focus on creating unity. Seldom do they criticize; instead they connect with people on both parties and look for ways to make things positive. Ronald Reagan comes to mind as a good example of a people connector. Now, this is not a book about politics, nor does it matter which political view you represent; I'm just using political leaders as the obvious example. Division occurs in companies, non-profit organizations, and religious groups. In fact, any time there is a group with certain characteristics that identify that group, there is potential for division from other groups. It is a natural bias to focus on benefiting one's own group even at the expense of another.

Criticism does not bring people together, nor does it make someone want to see your point of view. Criticism is divisive. What brings people together is collaboration, common ground, understanding, respectful and peaceful conversations, clear vision and purpose, and earnest appeal.

Not only do different groups have potential for division, but different personality types do as well. Consider a large organization with many departments, such as technology, research, marketing, human resources, sales, customer service, compliance, and accounting. Each department has its own interests and objectives. Also, the people who work in these different departments have different personality types. Because of the various interests, objectives, and personality types, it is common for friction to exist between departments. This friction, caused by differences, can easily create division within an organization. A leader's job is to recognize this and work to create unity.

Birds of a feather...

I'm sure you've heard the saying, "Birds of a feather flock together." Simply put, we all tend to hang around people who are similar to ourselves. It naturally makes us feel more comfortable. But here's the deal. The people with whom you associate will rub off on you, no matter how much you think it's not so. They will affect your views, the way you think, and the decisions you make.

Are the people you hang around affecting your personal growth? Are they providing fuel for your growth, or are they holding you back? Only you know the answer. And whatever the answer, only you can do something about it.

Without beating a dead horse, if you want to improve your character, you may need to change the characters you hang around.

Personal Growth

Developing character is pursued through personal growth. Personal growth occurs from a desire to grow and a willingness to learn. It is developed through self-discipline and self-control.

You can start learning about personal growth by reading books and attending seminars. But personal growth won't happen by solely reading a book or attending seminars—growth comes from applying what you learn, as well as daily, repetitive practice. For growth habits to stick for the long-term it takes consistent reinforcement. You must intentionally practice the new habit every single day in order for it to become part of what you do. It may take 21 days or it may take a year. But if it's important enough to you, then stick to it.

Sometimes it's helpful to have someone to whom you're accountable. This person could be an associate who desires to grow as well. You could have weekly meetings, by phone or in person, to share your past week—what worked and what didn't. Then discuss what you plan to do over the next week before your next meeting. Just knowing that you've got to share what you actually accomplished over the past week is motivation to get out there and do it. It might be a little embarrassing to come to the meeting each week having done nothing at all.

Other accountability methods may include working with a mentor or a coach. If you know of someone who is a leader and of good character, you might consider asking them if they'd be willing to work with you for a few minutes each week. Another option is to work with a coach who is trained in the area that you want to grow.

Practicing personal growth is an all-the-time thing, not just something you do when you're in a slump. When you practice during the smooth times, then you'll be better prepared during the rough times.

Questions for Growth

1. What triumphs have shaped who you are?
2. What adversity has shaped who you are?

3. How can you use your triumphs and adversity for personal growth?
4. How have choices affected who and where you are today?
5. How does your character affect your ability to connect?
6. How do you promote unity among others, including different groups?
7. How could you improve on your ability to promote unity?
8. Who are the closest people you hang around?
9. Are the people you hang around influencing you for growth or are they holding you back?
10. Do you need to change who you hang around?
11. Are you willing to read a book on personal growth? If so, where would you like to start?
12. Are you willing to work with an accountability partner, a mentor, or coach on personal growth? Who can you think of?
13. Is there a personal growth or leadership training you could attend?
14. What is your plan for personal growth? Write your plan and keep it in front of you daily. Intentionally work your plan and stick to it.

References and Sources:

Kouzes, James M. And Posner, Barry Z., *Learning Leadership: The Five Fundamentals of Becoming an Exemplary Leader* (Wiley 2016), chapter 4-You Have To Believe In Yourself, 33-43.

31

LEAD BY EXAMPLE

When my son Cole was in the first grade, the teacher sent home a worksheet the kids had done in class. The worksheet had a sticky note from the teacher that said, *"The school counselor wants to make sure you see this."*

My wife was like, "Oh my gosh! This is so embarrassing."

I was more like, "Oh my gosh, what the heck did he do this time?"

So I started reading the worksheet. The title of the worksheet was *"When I grow up I want to be _____."* Below the title there were four questions related to what the child wanted to be. Here's how Cole answered the questions.

For the title, "What do you want to be when you grow up?" Cole wrote, "A pilot."

The first question was, "Why is that a fun job?" Cole wrote, "You get to fly a plane."

The second question was, "Why will this job be hard?" Cole wrote, "But it will be hard to fly a plane."

The third question was, "What tools will you need to do this job?" Cole wrote, "A plane."

As my wife and I read those first three questions and Cole's answers we were thinking, "So far so good. These answers are pretty typical of a first grader."

Then I read the last question out loud, 'What do you want to do with your first paycheck?"

The answer was covered up with the sticky note from the teacher. I was thinking perhaps Cole wanted to buy an Xbox, a motorcycle, or a cool car since these are the things he regularly talks about.

I looked at my wife and she had her eyes closed. I said, "What are doing?"

She said, "Praying it's something good."

It wasn't.

When I lifted up the sticky note to reveal Cole's answer I fully understood why the school counselor wanted us to see this worksheet. I didn't read his answer aloud, I just moved the paper over so my wife and I could see it at the same time.

The fourth and final question was "What do you want to do with your first paycheck?"

Cole wrote—*buy some beer.*

It was at this point I fully realized what it means to *lead by example.* I know this story makes it sound like I'm a lush, but I'm not. Cole was at the age where he asked a lot of questions, like "Why can't kids drink beer?" "Why is beer only for adults?" "What does it taste like?" He was naturally curious. But he was also at an impressionable young age.

You never really know who is watching you and what they're watching. This is the nature of leadership. Whether you are aware or not, you are influencing someone, somehow, right now. This is why leadership is not just something you do while you're "in character." Leadership is not just something you do in your role, leadership is in *you.* You are the leader, not your position.

Being a leader doesn't mean you have to be perfect, not that you could be in the first place. It means being aware of your words and your actions. When you're aware of the things you say and do, hopefully you will be more mindful of how your words and actions might influence others. Maybe there are some things you need to do differently or things you need to stop doing. Maybe there are things you need to say differently or stop saying altogether. This will be for you to determine and decide.

But make no mistake, whether you consider yourself a leader or not, you are influencing someone right now. Sometimes it's the things you say, and sometimes it's the things you don't say. Sometimes it's the things you do, and sometimes it's the things you don't do. Leading by example is a full-time gig. Or with more emphasis, it's a full-time *responsibility.*

So what will make you a better leader?

A book is a good place to learn, but reading a book won't make you a leader. A seminar is a good place to learn, but attending a seminar won't make you a leader. There's only one thing that will help you develop into a leader—practice. Here are some examples.

- ➢ How does one become a good guitarist? Practice.
- ➢ How do you get good at math? Practice.
- ➢ How do you become a better reader or writer? Practice.
- ➢ How do you become a better public speaker? Practice.

Too often people start something only to find that it is difficult, then they quit. Playing a guitar is not easy. Learning math is not easy. Learning to read and write take time. Learning to do public speaking and overcoming the fear associated with it are not easy. All of these things and anything else that you desire to do or become will take time and practice. The more you practice, the better you'll become. All people who are great at anything were, at one time, beginners. Sure, some things come easier for some people than others. However, no matter your natural ability, becoming really good at something requires persistent practice.

If there's something you want to do, whether it's to become a leader, play an instrument, learn math, write a book, become a public speaker, or anything else you can imagine, decide to do it, then start doing it. You may not be all that good at first, in fact, you may be awful at whatever it is. But don't give up trying; the more you practice the better you will become.

Anything worth doing will probably be difficult, otherwise, everyone would be doing it. Just because it seems difficult, or even downright impossible at times, keep going. Too many people quit things too soon. Don't give up too soon. Go ahead and make a commitment to a certain time frame. If it's playing guitar, commit to taking lessons weekly and practicing 30 minutes a day. Make a short video of yourself trying to play guitar before your first lesson. Then make another video every month. At the end of a year you'll have thirteen videos. Watch them in order. If you've taken a weekly lesson and practiced 30 minutes a day, I think you'll be surprised at how far you've come. Keep going; make the commitment for another year.

Once you've made the commitment for a certain time period, break it down into small steps. Henry Ford said,

Nothing is particularly hard if you divide it into small jobs.

Continuing the example of playing guitar, get good at one note, then add another. Once you've learned the notes, learn a chord. Get good at one chord, then add another. Almost anything you want to learn can be broken down into small steps. At first you may think you could never play the guitar. But, can you learn one note? If you can learn one note, then you can learn two notes, and so on. (Side note—I do not play guitar, but my son does.)

Leadership works the same way. If it's your leadership skills that you want to improve, then start by making a commitment for a certain time period—at least a year. Next, decide where you want to start. Do you need to improve your people skills? More specifically, do you need to become a better listener or communicator? Choose one area to improve at first, then focus your learning and practicing on that one thing. If it's listening skills, get a book or attend a training on improving your listening skills. Then start practicing what you learn, every day.

Think of all your connections as the people you potentially influence. Some of these people may have a lower positional ranking than you, like your kids, employees, or the people you manage. However, some of them might have a higher positional ranking than you, like your parents, your employer, or your manager. Position does not matter when it comes to influence. Don't think for a second that you can't influence someone who has a higher position than you—you can and you do. Anyone and everyone who knows you, sees you, or hears you is someone you can potentially influence. And it all starts with your example. How *will* they see you? What example are you demonstrating? Is your example a positive one? Is it of good character? Are you the example you want to be? The example you set is totally your choice.

To wind this up, leadership is about connections. Everything you do and say influences your connections. The more connections you make, the more people you will influence. And, the deeper your connections, the better your relationships.

I'm not perfect by any means, and neither will you be perfect. Leadership is not about being perfect; leadership is about improvement. And everyone can do it, everyone can learn it, and everyone has room to grow.

Go ahead, lead the way.

Questions for Growth

1. Do you see yourself as an example?
2. To whom are you an example?
3. How can you improve your example?
4. If leadership is about improvement, what area would you like to improve about yourself?
5. If time wasn't an issue and if there were no obstacles, is there anything that you'd really like to do, become, or learn?
6. If there was one first step to doing the thing you want to do, becoming what you want to become, or learning what you want to learn, what would that first step be?
7. Is there anything holding you back from taking that first step?
8. If there is something holding you back, how could you move forward anyway?
9. If you could be any type of example you want to be, perhaps even to someone in particular, what kind of example would you be?

ABOUT THE AUTHOR

Bil Sadler, with a background in public accounting and financial services since 1991, shares experiences in performance, particularly leadership and service, through speaking, seminars, workshops, and training programs. Bil's credentials include Certified Public Accountant, CFP® practitioner, Chartered Financial Analyst, and Independent Certified Coach, Trainer, and Speaker of The John Maxwell Certification Program.

NEED A SPEAKER?

For more information about booking Bil for speaking, breakout sessions, workshops, seminars, or training, visit:
bilsadler.com

Made in the USA
Columbia, SC
14 April 2019